Ulick O'Connor's biographies include *Oliver St John Gogarty*, *Brendan Behan* and the much praised *Celtic Dawn* — a biographical portrait of the Irish literary renaissance. He is further known as a poet and playwright, and has published three books of verse, as well as verse plays. O'Connor's one-man show on Brendan Behan was performed by the author himself and produced in Britain, Europe and the US, and a recent off-Broadway production of *Joyicity* was a major success; his play *Execution* still holds the record for the longest run of a new play at the Abbey Theatre. He has lectured widely in the US and Ireland on literature, theatre and biography.

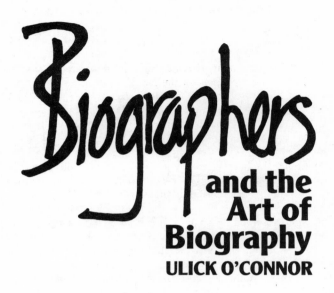

Biographers

and the
Art of
Biography

ULICK O'CONNOR

QUARTET BOOKS

For A.J.F., buttie and friend,
'parfit gentil knyght' of the oval game

First published in paperback by Quartet Books Limited 1993
A member of the Namara Group
27/29 Goodge Street
London W1P 1FD

A catalogue record for this title is available
from the British Library

ISBN 0 7043 0177 6

Typeset by The Electronic Book Factory Ltd, Fife, Scotland
Printed and bound in Great Britain by BPCC Hazells Ltd
Member of BPCC Ltd

Acknowledgements

I would like to thank Enda Hogan and the Irish Permanent Building Society for their sponsorship which enabled me to complete this book. I am grateful to Professor Terence Brown and Professor Nicholas Grene of the English Department at Trinity College, Dublin, who arranged for the lectures which I gave on 'The Biographer as Artist' at Trinity College, Dublin, in the autumn of 1987. Dr Trevor West of the same university lent me his usual valuable support.

I am deeply indebted to Lelia O'Flaherty for undertaking the daunting task of editing the extensive quotations and references which a book of this kind demands.

I would also like to express my deep gratitude to Gerard O'Flaherty who has been my helmsman guiding me through many difficult currents. I was particularly fortunate to have the advice of Dr Liberato Santoro of the Philosophy Department of University College, Dublin. Though he combines a wide knowledge of scholastic philosophy with a keen awareness and sensitivity to literature, he never allowed his enthusiasm to sway his judgement whenever I put an aesthetic problem before him. Timothy Mooney was also most helpful in this area.

Jane Knechtel rendered heroic work on footnotes and bibliography in difficult conditions, for which I would like to thank her.

Typing a manuscript of this kind is always difficult and I would like to acknowledge the help of Pat Nolan, Lynn Kemp and Darinia Diskin.

Seamus Cashman has encouraged me over the past three years in the writing of this book and patiently waited as revised versions followed, one after the other.

Contents

	Foreword to this Edition	ix
	Preface	xi
Chapter 1	Selector or Collector	1
Chapter 2	To Tell or Not To Tell	46
Chapter 3	Who Dares Wins	59
Chapter 4	The Biographer's Way	70
Chapter 5	Personal Record	90
	Epilogue	104
Appendices	1 The Good and the Beautiful	107
	2 Getting at the Facts	114
Notes		127
Select Bibliography		138
Index		144

Foreword to this Edition

Since Harold Nicolson's *The Development of English Biography* (1929) there has been comparatively little work published in English on the subject. In the United States Leon Edel has written an impressive study *Writing Lives: Principia Biographia*, while in the early sixties Dr James L. Clifford edited a significant collection of essays which included three seminal ones by Virginia Woolf later published in *Granite and Rainbow* (1958). There have also been a number of academic studies in the United States and Britain. But it was the recent increasing interest in biography that led me to believe that there was room for further examination of the range and possibilities of the form.

Since the first edition of *Biographers and the Art of Biography* two years ago there has been no sign of a decrease in public fascination with the genre. Controversies surrounding biographies in the last twelve months (Andrew Motion's forthcoming *Philip Larkin* and Hugh David's *Stephen Spender*) have featured in the newspaper headlines, and been the subject of discussions on radio and TV chat shows. The decision in the case of the Cambridge biography of D. H. Lawrence to have it written under multiple authorship has also caused widespread debate.

At the Dartington Literature Festival in August 1992, one of the themes selected was 'The Art of Biography'. Fiona McCarthy (the biographer of Eric Gill), Frances Spalding (biographer of Vanessa Bell and John Minton), Kathleen Jones (biographer of Christina Rossetti), Andrew Motion and the present author were among those who spoke.

A question which arose more than once in discussion at Dartington Hall was how far the biographer can go in allowing his reader to participate in all the information available to him. Fiona McCarthy talked about the problem of including in her biography of Eric Gill revelations about the incestuous relationship between Gill and his daughter. Andrew Motion, reading from the manuscript of his biography of Philip Larkin, presented a startling portrait of Larkin's father as a pre-war Nazi supporter who kept a statue of Hitler in his room in Coventry Town Hall, when he was City Treasurer. Asked whether the inclusion of such material might not have repercussions on friends and relatives of Larkin, Motion made it clear that he considered its inclusion was justified in the context of the overall structure of the biography.

My own view, which I expressed in a round-table discussion with Motion, Frances Spalding and Kathleen Jones (and which relates to a dominant theme in this book), was that any suppression of fact for reasons unconnected with the shaping of a biographical portrait is no part of the biographer's task. If the biographer approaches his work in the context of a work of art, as a painter or sculptor should, he will have no difficulty in relegating or elevating to its proper position material which used in another context might give offence.

This book is an examination of the principles underlying biography as an art form, and an attempt to establish criteria which will enable us to distinguish between such an approach and that which confines itself to mere chronicling and presentation of the facts.

Preface

In his essay on Proust, Samuel Beckett has identified a dilemma facing the contemporary writer. ' "Man", writes Proust, "is not a building that can receive additions to its superficies, but a tree whose stem and leafage are an expression of inward sap." We are alone. We cannot know and we cannot be known. "Man is the creature that cannot come forth from himself, who knows others only in himself, and who, if he asserts the contrary, lies." '[1]

Are we to conclude then that the Romantic movement has reached its ebb? Is the journey into self which began with Rousseau and Voltaire, and continued through Baudelaire and Camus, at a dead end? In fact can we escape at all from time – 'that double-headed monster of damnation and salvation' – to represent the real? Are writers harlequins playing at best with masks? Is fiction falling into disrepute, because of a fear that it cannot represent what is at the root of the modern conscience?

Adopting a less pessimistic stance, I have tried to assess whether the remobilization of fact in a creative context through biography can provide an answer to the epistemological dilemma posed above.

One night in Tangier while engaged on a work of biography I had a chance insight into how technology may assist the writer to extend the possibilities inherent in writing factual narrative. I was having dinner with Paul Bowles, the novelist, in his apartment on the outskirts of the town. We talked of James Jones, the American evangelist who had persuaded over nine hundred people of different social backgrounds, doctors, lawyers, journalists, working class, to surrender their incomes to him and take up residence in the Guyanan jungle in an attempt to form a commune. The experiment never reached any adequate stage of development because after two years, angered by the interference of what he thought were hostile forces, Jones, now half demented, ordered his followers to kill themselves in a mass suicide pact. For eight hours, nine hundred people stood in line to accept a cup of death from their leader, and as their bodies fell writhing on the ground they were replaced by new devotees anxious to follow out Jones's instructions.

Bowles's conversation is conducted in low key. He tends to make his observations in a carefully modulated voice. But now he said with (for him) some excitement: 'Did you ever hear Jones's laugh?'

He went into his bedroom and emerged with a cassette player and a tape on which had been recorded an address Jones had made to his 'congregation' some weeks before his death. After some preliminary pressing of buttons he finally came to where Jones at the conclusion of one of his maniacal announcements began to laugh. One heard a sound like nothing one had ever heard before. It was the whine of the ego in unrestrained triumph over whatever remained of the intellect. There was a high cruel note to it like the engine of a submarine. It continued to rise in pitch till it seemed beyond the range of what the vocal chords can ordinarily achieve and touched some element in the psyche that one had never sensed before.

'Isn't that something?' said Bowles in his normal calm

voice. He was good enough to make a copy of the tape and I have listened to it many times since then.

It seemed to me that in that laugh was contained the outward expression of the 'inward sap'. There beyond the deformity of time and habit lay the key to that 'inaccessible dungeon' which holds the essence the writer seeks to represent. No matter how a biographer has submerged himself in archive or interview he should keep such incidents before the mind's eye – work from the inside out. Having reached the source he should tap it, let it flow where it will, and thus released from the captivity of chronology, may achieve a work of art.

1

Selector or Collector

In this examination of the biographer's function I would not wish the reader to conclude that all of the arguments I shall deal with have only become relevant in the context of contemporary biography. No, many of the controversies which engage biographers today have been the subject of debate for a very long time indeed. For instance, one of the more loathsome devices to emerge in recent times has been 'faction', where the writer dispenses himself from the disciplines of biographical science, and invents conversations between his subject and other persons who appear in the narrative. He can even go so far as to create situations which, if not in actual conflict with the facts, certainly have no provenance in existing source material.

Yet as far back as the ninth century we can find an eminent ecclesiastic engaged in similar manoeuvres. He however does offer the excuse that he is resorting to this device on the grounds of a special relationship with the Divinity, which to their credit even the modern proponents of the genre have not claimed so far. The Bishop of Ravenna, writing about 823, and purporting to record the life stories of his predecessors, was not at all deterred by 'gaps' in the material available –

1

> In order that there might not be a break in the series,
> I have composed the life myself, with the help of God
> and the prayers of the brethren.[1]

Then, too, in most discussions of biography from Plutarch to the present day, there is a tendency I believe to give too much credit to Boswell as innovator. Undoubtedly his inexhaustible energy and the precision with which he noted down the conversation of a great man of letters have helped to mould a biographical portrait which is generally considered a work of art. But while the personalized record of individual conversations had little significance in the factual historical narratives of Boswell's contemporaries, one has only to go back a century and a half or so to find a similar technique made use of by an impecunious Elizabethan archivist-archaeologist. John Aubrey's lack of funds had led him to cultivate special gifts, so that he had acquired by middle life the status of what we would today term a professional house guest. His diaries, which he modestly entitled *Brief Lives*, can give us flashes of insight into the personalities of the people he met, and heard talked about, which a volume of contemporary chronicles might fail to achieve. For instance, in his *Brief Lives* he has less than nine hundred words concerning Henry VIII's Lord Chancellor, Sir Thomas More. But his portrait is shaped like a Matisse drawing – every line says something, nothing superfluous is left in. Yet the pragmatism, energy and invention which were at the root of Thomas More's character could hardly be better portrayed than in Aubrey's splendid sketch.

> Sir Thomas More, Lord Chancellour: his Countrey-howse was at Chelsey, in Middlesex, where Sir John Danvers built his howse ... On this place the Lord Chancellour More was wont to recreate himself and contemplate. It happened one time that a Tom of Bedlam came up to him, and had a Mind to have throwne him from the battlements, saying Leap, Tom,

leap. The Chancellour was in his gowne, and besides ancient and not able to struggle with such a strong fellowe. My Lord had a little dog. Sayd he: Let us first throwe the dog downe, and see what sporte that will be. So the dog was throwne over. This is very fine sporte, sayd my Lord, Let us fetch him up, and try once more. While the mad man was goeing downe, my Lord fastned the dore, and called for help, but ever after kept the dore shutt.[2]

A second anecdote of Aubrey's (whose source was his friend Mris Tyndale) perfectly illustrates the consistency which dominated Sir Thomas More's life, whether as one of the great jurists in English Law or as a future canonized saint who would choose the gallows rather than compromise his conscience.

In his *Utopia* his lawe is that the young people are to see each other stark-naked before marriage. Sir William Roper, of Eltham, in Kent, came one morning, pretty early, to my Lord, with a proposall to marry one of his daughters. My Lord's daughters were then both together abed in a truckle-bed in their father's chamber asleep. He carries Sir William into the chamber and takes the Sheete by the corner and suddenly whippes it off. They lay on their Backs, and their smocks up as high as their armepitts. This awakened them, and immediately they turned on their bellies. Quoth Roper, I have seen both sides, and so gave a patt on the buttock he made choice of, sayeing, Thou art mine. Here was all the trouble of the wooeing.[3]

No, Boswell did not initiate the possibilities of anecdotal and personalized conversation as an ingredient for the biographer — rather he extended them.

During the nineteenth century, the battle about the position of the biographer rolled back and forth — but mostly backwards. Lockhart in his massive and unreadable life of Scott declared he had no intention of being what he described as 'Boswellized'. He refused to make use, however illustrative they might be of the personality of his subject, of the contents of the numerous conversations he had with Sir Walter Scott. Even Wordsworth, once herald of a revolution which purported to establish freedom of speech, would question the propriety of revealing details about an author's private life. For a historical figure yes! But a writer's peccadilloes were no business of the public and were better left out. Tennyson was no better on the matter.

> What business has the public to know about Byron's wildnesses? He has given them fine work and they ought to be satisfied.[4]

With poets condoning censorship it was not to be expected that the shackles binding biography would be easily lifted from the writers' shoulders. A series of unreadable biographies such as Moore's two-volume life of Byron, his life of Sheridan, Forster's three-volume life of Dickens and Trevelyan's life of Macaulay are indications of the disarray into which the form had fallen.

By the time John Morley came to write his life of Gladstone it would have been hoped that the situation would have changed. Twice Chief Secretary for Ireland in Gladstone's government, he had been in the intimate confidence of the Grand Old Man, and had been his chief assistant in steering the Second Home Rule Bill through the House of Commons. Besides he was a journalist of great repute who had changed the *Pall Mall Gazette* from a conservative right-wing paper into a radical one and had written studies of Voltaire and Rousseau. In particular, he had, as a result of his early experience as a journalist, a knowledge of shorthand, which would have enabled him, so to speak, to 'Boswellize' his subject and collect valuable material for an intimate portrait.

But alas, when the statutory three-volume work emerged, it was bereft of the personality of his subject

– a monument to factual accuracy but a warning to anyone who would attempt to impose the approach of the biographer as artist on his volumes. Ironically, in the last of the three volumes John Morley has casually inserted a few pages entitled 'Table Talk' which allow us a tantalizing glimpse of what the biography might have become if the material had been handled in another way. Clearly, by reason of its position in the work and the way it is presented, Morley did not consider Gladstone's table talk significant and probably only added it lest some tit-bit might elude the maw of posterity.

But it is certainly not the stuff of gossip that we encounter when Gladstone poses to Morley the question: 'Which century of English history produced the greatest men?'

J.M. –   What do you say to the sixteenth?

Mr. G. –   Yes I think so. Gardiner was a great man. Henry VIII was great. But bad. Poor Cranmer. Like Northcote he'd no backbone. Do you remember Jeremy Collier's sentence about his bravery at the stake, which I count one of the grandest in English prose – 'He seemed to repel the force of the fire and to overlook the torture, by strength of thought.' Thucydides could not beat that . . .

The old man twice declaimed the sentence with deep sonorous voice, and his usual incomparable modulation.'[5]

Now Gladstone's own life had been distinguished by strength of character and moral purpose – and the discovery of his affection for Collier's phrase, 'to repel the force of the fire and to overlook the torture by strength of thought', is something which could have been seized on by a biographer anxious to bring us in contact with the personality of a prime minister who held under his control the destiny of the most powerful country in the world. But no such comment intrudes itself in Morley's account.

Here are Morley's notes for a luncheon on 4 January 1892:

> At luncheon, Mr Gladstone recalled the well-known story of Talleyrand on the death of Napoleon. The news was brought when T. chanced to be dining with Wellington. "Quel événement!" they all cried. "Non, ce n'est pas un événement," said Talleyrand, "c'est une nouvelle" – 'Tis no event, 'tis a piece of news. "Imagine such a way," said Mr G., "of taking the disappearance of that colossal man! Compare it with the opening of Manzoni's ode, which makes the whole earth stand still. Yet both points of view are right. In one sense, the giant's death was only news; in another, when we think of his history, it was enough to shake the world." At the moment he could not recall Manzoni's words, but at dinner he told me that he had succeeded in piecing them together, and after dinner he went to his room and wrote them down for me on a piece of paper. Curiously enough, he could not recall the passage in his own splendid translation.[6]

What does this tell us? First of all Gladstone's assessment of a man who had been his own country's probable conqueror, when Gladstone was still a boy. (He was twenty-five when the death of the French Emperor took place.) Then his knowledge of Manzoni's poem and his admiration for it recalls the young politician caught up in the exhilaration of the great wave of freedom that swept Italy and the greater part of Europe in the middle of the nineteenth century.

Yet there is still no comment from Morley. He remains the shorthand notetaker sitting in the House of Commons whose function is to provide for the daily reader a record of what has happened and no more. Morley admits that it is not easy to define 'the charm of these [Mr. Gladstone's] conversations'.[7] Is charm the right word? They are in the highest degree stimulating, bracing, informative and their casual positioning in this three-volume tome is in itself an indictment of the approach of the Victorian school of biography.

Morley in relegating such matters to the status of gossip has failed in one of the first tasks of the biographer — to provide his reader with an insight into the personality as well as the achievement of the subject; Moore in his two-volume *Life* of his friend Byron, a fearful edifice of the 'Life and Letters' variety, left it to the last four pages to give us a personalized description of the man we had been reading about for the preceding 500 pages, a procedure which, if adopted at the beginning of the work, would have kept before the eye of the reader as the narrative unfolded an image of the poet's physical appearance as perceived by a close friend.[8]

Then with the twentieth century a new situation confronted the biographer. The great Victorian revolution in thought had weakened categorical beliefs in religion and nationalism. The discoveries of the psychiatric schools had shown that it is within himself rather than the exterior world that the human being may come to terms with his own personality — may discover his relation to his environment. Then with the coming of the post-war era, accelerated perhaps by the imminence of a nuclear holocaust and the new dimension created by the discovery of the extermination camps, the concept of existential man emerged — man responsible for himself. But having renounced his crutches, he found a new manner of walking had to be devised — and there is little evidence so far that a satisfactory equilibrium has been achieved.

It is evident, however, that life outside categories is less likely to lend itself to plot. So the dive into self in the hope of revealing an uncharted world, 'the unconscious psychic life of the soul',[9] might provide a higher quality of experience than that formerly engendered by inventive narrative. If this is so, by allying the scaffolding of fact to the imaginative faculty, some form might emerge which could exceed the potential of the novel. Such a form would require a new concept of biography quite different in quality from that adopted by the writers of the nineteenth century two-volume tome. Among the outstanding pioneers who were to lead this revolutionary approach to biography were an Englishman and a Frenchman, Lytton Strachey and André Maurois.

Strachey set out his approach in a famous passage in the preface to *Eminent Victorians*.

> It is not by the direct method of a scrupulous narration that the explorer of the past can hope to depict that singular epoch. If he is wise, he will adopt a subtler strategy. He will attack his subject in unexpected places; he will fall upon the flank, or the rear; he will shoot a sudden, revealing searchlight into obscure recesses, hitherto undivined. He will row out over that great ocean of material, and lower down into it, here and there, a little bucket, which will bring up to the light of day some characteristic specimen, from those far depths, to be examined with a careful curiosity.[10]

So Strachey was saying that while the biographer must not ignore the vast amount of knowledge now available to him, he must still select from it with the discretion of the artist if he is to achieve a true portrait.

Here was undoubtedly the approach of the artist. It was clear also from the nature of the writing itself that Strachey was in a position to fulfil the expectations he had given the reader in setting out his principles of work. In his three great biographies, *Eminent Victorians, Elizabeth and Essex*[11] and *Queen Victoria,*[12] occur passage after passage of splendid prose which proclaim the artist in words as well as the chronicler of events. Take, for instance, this passage on the distinction between Elizabeth and her rival Philip of Spain:

> In spite of superficial resemblances, she was the very opposite of her most dangerous enemy — the weaving spider of the Escurial. Both were masters of dissimulation and lovers of delay; but the leaden foot of Philip was the symptom of a dying organism, while Elizabeth temporised for the contrary reason — because vitality can afford to wait. The fierce old hen sat still, brooding over the English nation, whose pullulating energies were coming swiftly to ripeness and unity under her wings. She sat still; but every feather bristled; she was tremendously alive.[13]

We can feel that liveliness leaping off the page. In France André Maurois was proceeding along similar lines with his life of Shelley in which he set out to arrange authentic material in the manner of a novel and give his reader the feeling of his character's progressive discovery of the world which is the essence of romance. Maurois was quite frank in his ambition to transcend the craftsman in his approach to biography. Referring to his life of Balzac,[14] Maurois tells us of his intentions when he wishes to communicate to the reader in his biography the elements of a work of art.

> I want the reader to feel at times that he is in Balzac's own workroom, possessed of the same rich memories, at the moment when that blazing fusion occurs from which emerge *Le Père Goriot* or *Une Fille d'Eve*. If I have succeeded, if the reader participates a little in the life of Balzac and in the Balzacian creation, then I have won . . .[15]

As with Strachey, Maurois demonstrates that he himself is a master of prose. Take this passage from his biography of Marcel Proust. Not only does it show a perception of the artist's role in literature, but it is expressed in such a way that it amply demonstrates that the biographer himself has the potential for such a role.

> It is not enough to observe. The artist must penetrate beyond the object, beyond the creatures of flesh and blood, to the mysterious truths concealed in them. Beauty is like those fairy-tale princesses who have been shut up in a castle by some mighty magician. We may, after much striving, open a thousand doors and yet not find them, and most men, urged forward by the active enthusiasms of youth, tire of the search and soon abandon it. But a Proust will sacrifice everything in order to reach imprisoned loveliness, and a day of revelation comes at last, of illumination and of certainty, when he finds his glittering and concealed reward.[16]

But if Strachey and Maurois had invented or perceived an art form, there was one branch of the biographical science which they tended to underrate, that of the personal interview. It could be argued that Strachey could hardly have spoken to an intimate of the Virgin Queen, or Maurois ferreted out in a Parisian garret some contemporary of Balzac. But Strachey when he wrote *Eminent Victorians* could certainly have spoken with contemporaries of General Gordon, or Cardinal Manning, and that he did not do so at least in the case of General Gordon takes from his final portrait.

But this gap in the biographical method was to be remedied with a vengeance after the Second World War. Perhaps the invention of the tape recorder has made the interviewing process easier and more productive of accuracy than hitherto – or perhaps the facility with which one might now travel from place to place, or the general willingness of people in the second half of the century to talk more about the habits and hidden peculiarities of people whom they have known, may have contributed to this phenomenon. Whatever it was, in the post-Second World War period a number of biographers began to use the personal interview (in addition to archival material), not simply as a basis for their study, but in such a way as to dominate the treatment of their subject as it emerged in the final work. These diligent investigators may have had in mind Dr Johnson's well-known pronouncement as a justification for their approach.

> ... more knowledge may be gained of a man's real character, by a short conversation with one of his servants, than from a formal and studied narrative, begun with his pedigree and ended with his funeral.[17]

But the problem was that, no matter how interesting the content of the interviews, if it didn't relate in some way to the final portrait it had no place in a work of art. The biographer was not dispensed from his role as an artist (as envisaged by Strachey and Maurois) if he simply presented his reader with vast collections of information. There still remained the duty – to choose. James L. Clifford, the critic and biographer, has summed up the dilemma of the new biographer as follows:

> What, really, is a biographer? Is he merely a superior kind of journalist, or must he be an artist? Is writing a life a narrow branch of history or a form of literature? Or may it be something in between, a strange amalgam of science and art? The difference between a craftsman and an artist is obvious. The one knows exactly what his product will be. He works with specific materials and uses traditional techniques. His skill comes as a result of serious study and long practice. The other works intuitively, evolving each move that he makes, and not certain until the end just what his work will be. Originality and genius are more important than practice. Is the life-writer one or the other, or both?[18]

What Dr Clifford is saying here is that either the biographer approaches his task as a craft, or else he casts himself perilously on the sea of the imagination and seeks to produce a work of art. It is somewhat the same distinction that Thomas Aquinas makes between the good and the beautiful, and which could be used as a working structure for the proposition we are going to examine here.

For Aquinas the act of cognition involves satisfaction or content when the perception of form through matter is achieved by the mind. This is *bonum* or the good. *'Bonum est quod omnia appetunt'* (The good is what all desire). It is the mind's function to abstract form from matter and when this occurs the mind is satisfied. But when, in the process of abstraction, the mind is spared the least difficulty by the harmonious relations of the parts to one another, as occurs in the perception of the beautiful, then, in addition to being satisfied, the mind is also pleased. It has had an easy ride, so to speak. *'Pulchra enim dicuntur quae visa placent'* (We call beautiful those things which give pleasure when they are seen) or *'Pulchrum autem dicatur id cuius ipsa apprehensio placet'* (Let that be called beautiful the very perception of which pleases).[19]

So, to take Dr Clifford a stage further, by the application of these rules we could say that the biographer of either the nineteenth-century 'factual' variety, or the more modern one in which either the personal interview or the use of archival material, letters, diaries, reports, are used without any special selection process taking place, is a craftsperson who deals with the *bonum* or the good – while the biographer who would approach his subject through the intuitive process of selection is hoping to ally himself with *pulchrum* or the beautiful, and thus achieve a work of art.

First, perhaps we should examine the approach of those modern biographers who deal with the *bonum* – who supply us with the information, often amassed with prodigious energy and tenacity, which they use to chronicle the life of their subject without involving themselves in the selective process. Among the first of these interviewers-scholars to make an impact on the world of biography was Professor Ellmann with his biography of James Joyce, first published in 1959.[20] Arriving in Dublin in the early fifties to begin his work, this graduate of Yale University interviewed many hundreds of people who had personally known Joyce or knew the period in which he lived.

His energy was indefatigable. Legends grew up of how with Sherlock Holmes-like tenacity he tracked down minutiae that enabled him to identify the original of a character in *Dubliners* or *Ulysses*, or how he had managed to discover the whereabouts of school friends and acquaintances of Joyce at University College, Dublin, who had confided to him fascinating information about the doings of the artist as a young man. Nor were we led to believe that Ellmann's industry had stopped here. He had travelled widely in Switzerland, Italy and France in search of people who would have recollections of Joyce during the different stages of his career. The result is a book which is one of the most readable of modern biographies. The narrative technique is cleverly constructed and we are led along through the different stages of Joyce's life with the ease with which a practised novelist brings his reader through his fictional routes.

But at the end of it all is there not a difficulty about this approach? We have been told so much about Joyce that some of us might be forgiven for wondering, in the process, have we grasped the essence of the real man. If everything is thrown in, then the discretion by which the biographer should establish himself as an artist by creating a work of the imagination has been abandoned. Despite the appetizing information that greets us in chapter after chapter, do we have an enriched knowledge of the personality of a writer who produced the greatest prose in English this century; or are we left with a somewhat bland image, no different in substance from that found in the numerous academic studies and biographical sketches which have already appeared?

Now it has to be said that the argument has been made with much force by a number of reputable critics, that Professor Ellmann's approach to biography presents us with a prodigious mass of material agreeably arranged, and it is up to the reader to select and form his own picture of Joyce from the material provided. Everyman his own artist, so to speak. But while this is in some ways an attractive approach in view of the contemporary tendency to undervalue the artist's role, and substitutes for it a more democratic status, it does not stand up, in my belief, on closer scrutiny. If Rembrandt, in his famous painting of the Musketeers of Captain Franz Banting Cocq, the *Militia of the Night Watch*, had followed such an approach and included in fine detail every aspect of the sitters before him, we would not have the masterpiece that we have today. When some of them complained subsequently that they had been relegated to the background, the artist's answer was that he was not simply seeking to present a conventional portrait, but to convey the excitement and agitation he sensed from the scene before him, and this could only be achieved by the arrangement he presented them with. It was a matter of shade and light. He did not allow the viewer the luxury of making up his own mind – he made it up for him by presenting him with a work stamped with the mark of genius, and which could only have one effect, that intended by the artist himself.

This is the sort of thinking that appears to have recommended itself to Strachey and Maurois in their attempt to impart to biography the character of a work of art. But Professor Ellmann has allied himself with the *bonum* or 'factual' school who do not feel impelled to activate the selective faculty, and I would argue in the process has diminished the possibility of achieving a definitive portrait.

To take a few examples. In his biography of James Joyce (p. 83n), Professor Ellmann credits an unknown poet, Paul Gregan, with having written some verses 'that may have helped Joyce in the writing of the final poem in *Chamber Music*, "I hear an army charging upon the land"'. Now if we look up this poem 'Recreant' by Gregan (it is not quoted by Professor Ellmann), we find that not only could it not have 'helped' Joyce, but if he *had* read it his reaction would have been likely to have been one of derision. Its last two verses run:

With snatches of barbaric battle-hymns,
And pagan spells of power and songs divine,
We sang where one pale red rose ever swims
Above a crystal shrine.

But if, amid the angry war, I go
To strike a chord of wild seraphic song,
God will forgive, the pale rose brighter glow
And beauty conquer wrong.

(from *Sunset Town*, Hermetic Society 1904)

To suggest (as Professor Ellmann does) that Joyce could have had 'an affinity' with such nonsense is ridiculous. But to assert that Gregan's verse could have any connection, however remote, with the writing of Joyce's 'I hear an army charging upon the land', with its halting rhythms, its half rhymes and plunges into the subconscious, is simply a failure in literary judgement. In this context Gregan does not belong in any biography of Joyce, and by planting him there Professor Ellmann has lessened rather than added to his portrait.

Then take Professor Ellmann's treatment of Joyce's relationship with his father. This was quite clearly an extremely close one. According to Joyce, his father 'thought and talked of me up to his last breath'. Joyce goes on to say that 'hundreds of pages and scores of characters in my books came from him'.[21]

Now Professor Ellmann does give us quite an amount of information indeed about the father and son in the last twenty years of John Stanislaus Joyce's life. But some of it is self-contradictory and there is no attempt to resolve the contradictions. Joyce would maintain somewhat dramatically that he could not return to Ireland to see his father, because of his foreboding that he would be undone there. But what was to stop Joyce bringing his father to Bognor in Sussex when he was on an extended visit there in 1923, or later to Torquay in Devon, a journey of about four hours from Dublin by ferry and hired car, which could have been undertaken at minimal cost? Indeed when he was staying at Bognor he received news of a gift from Harriet Weaver of £12,000 (£220,000 in today's money) and it would have been a not unfilial response for the son to have invited his father to England for a holiday on the strength of this windfall. But though he would receive in the next ten years from Miss Weaver a sum amounting in today's money to nearly half a million pounds (£438,000), he was not to use a penny of this towards making an attempt to see the parent to whom he owed so much. 'It is not his death that crushed me so much but self-accusation', he wrote to Harriet Weaver in January 1932.[22]

It is extraordinary that there is no comment from Professor Ellmann on this bizarre behaviour on Joyce's part. Yet as we read the material placed before us it is clear that some elucidation from a biographer, seeking to resolve the conflict of personality in his subject, is necessary. There was surely some deep psychological force at work preventing Joyce from meeting with his father. It could have been that he believed it would affect the delicate balance which enabled him to bring up, from his subconscious, material which would form the basis of what appeared in his work. It could be a sense of guilt at leaving his father behind in charge of a large family as he did. Perhaps the emotional shock would have been too great for him if he had met his father *en face*, and seen reflected there marks of those dreadful years, when the family of fourteen had led a gypsy-like existence through the labyrinth of the Dublin middle class. There are many grounds for speculation. But one thing a biographer should not do is to leave such matters hanging in the air without comment as Professor Ellmann has. The bald presentation of facts is not enough. It was Joyce himself who made the remark (when discussing *Plutarch's Lives* with Arthur Power) that mere accumulations of fact belong to the 'daylight of human personality'[23] but what the modern writer should concern himself with was 'exploring those undercurrents which flow beneath the apparently firm surface'.

While as I have said Professor Ellmann has been indefatigable in his unearthing of factual material relating to his subject there are nevertheless occasions when there have been inexplicable omissions. For instance we are given quite a lot of information about Nino Frank, the Italian journalist and writer. We learn (p.700) that he often accompanied Joyce to the movies, that he persuaded him to lend his name to the committee of a new literary magazine *Bifur* (p.615) and that he kept regularly in touch with Joyce. However, apart from (in a footnote on p.615) recording a remark made to him by Joyce expressing dislike of D.H. Lawrence's writing, and a rather bland description of some of their work done together on the translation of *Finnegans Wake* into Italian (of which we are given no excerpts), the general picture we are given of Frank is that of an agreeable literary hanger-on.

There is no hint at all that Frank has left behind (in *Souvenirs sur James Joyce*, La Table Ronde, 1949) an account of Joyce that is a biographer's dream. It is packed with what Joyce himself would have called 'epiphanies', the showing forth in a few words of aspects of personality, that put in another way might take chapters to achieve. His description of taking Joyce to see Samuel Beckett in hospital, after Beckett had been stabbed by a street tramp in Paris in 1937, and how the two Irish writers faced each other in the hospital room 'marinated in intolerable silences; from time to time they exchanged a few words, a short laugh', makes a vivid word picture. To Frank they seemed as 'two brothers, in their shape and their keenness like twin knifeblades'. By allying them with Swift he has achieved an acute insight into the modern Irish personality with its blending of Anglo-Irish and Gaelic elements.

> The elder and the younger were united by a profound bond, to find the explanation of which one need go no further than Swift or simply any postcard showing a Dublin pub, some shops, and the passers-by. Joyce confirmed my feeling when, having had enough of silences, we left. As we were returning to the Rue Edmond Valentin he openly made fun of his young friend's misadventure.
>
> 'He is truly Irish,' he told me. 'He doesn't hold it against the tramp at all, but do you know what he's mad about? The knife made a hole in his overcoat. He wants the judge to make it up to him and buy him another one.'[24]

Now there is no doubt that Professor Ellmann had met Nino Frank and there are notes from a number of interviews with him in the Joyce biography: and besides he had to hand the description of Joyce's visit to Beckett in hospital that I have described above. Why then should he have failed to make use of such a descriptive jewel for his biography? Perhaps he had already hauled in so much factual material, without having any special selective process in mind, that when he came to put together the final narrative the marvellous Nino Frank description simply slipped the net.

Do we then apply the phrase 'stuffed with truth' to Professor Ellmann's biography, as Virginia Woolf has used it to describe the biographies of Edward VII and Shakespeare written by Sir Sidney Lee? The first she tells us, because of its indiscriminate use of material, is unreadable and the second, for the same reason, dull.[25] Now Professor Ellmann's *James Joyce* could never be said to be either 'unreadable' or 'dull'.[25] His skilful arrangement of material, his flair for moving the narrative, his meticulous transcription of the dialogue of his interviews make his work, to use a popular phrase, an excellent read. But has he done what Mrs Woolf, in laying down guidelines for the new biography as created by Strachey or Maurois, claims is essential for its success – chosen 'those truths which transmit personality'?[26] The critic Hugh Kenner is adamant that Professor Ellmann has failed in this because he hasn't made us feel in his biography 'the presence of the mind that made the life worth writing and makes it worth reading'.[27]

Another writer who has provided enormous pleasure to those interested in contemporary biography is Michael Holroyd, who first became known for his life of the novelist Hugh Kingsmill, published in 1963. He then made a considerable impact with his massive two-volume work on Lytton Strachey (1968), stretching to nearly 1200 pages in all.[28]

There were indications, however, as one read through the Strachey biography that Mr Holroyd was perhaps succumbing to the same temptations as Professor Ellmann had in becoming the creature rather than the master of his material.

He has described vividly for us the roomfuls of documents, diaries, letters and manuscripts with which he was confronted when he was chosen by James

Strachey, Lytton's brother, to do the biography. This was a daunting task for someone who in his previous biography had tended to include rather than exclude when it came to dealing with the material on hand. Now faced with this vast colossus of fact, a new temptation, almost Mephistophelean, was added. He came into contact with Gerald Brenan, the author of notable books on Spain, who resided in that country and who turned out to have written love letters amounting to 400,000 words to Dora Carrington, that strange woman who was Lytton Strachey's confidant and aspiring lover. Brenan, although his base was in a remote Andalusian village, used to make frequent forays to London on amorous missions to Carrington and he generously made available (this despite the fact that he intended to publish in the near future his autobiography) not only the letters, but his journals of those vital years when all the sexual rigmarole surrounding Ham Spray, Lytton Strachey's country house, was in full swing. It was Brenan's journals and information which revealed the full scope of Dora Carrington's amorous mischief. Professing to be in love with the homosexual Strachey, she was at the same time capable of having prolonged and agonizing affairs with his acquaintances; such as Mark Gertler the painter, and Brenan himself. In the end Gertler gassed himself, but Brenan, of tougher breed, survived after Carrington had, as was her way, dismissed him.[29] You see we already have come quite a long way from Lytton Strachey. So perhaps does Mr Holroyd in his extended biography.

It could be argued that in widening his scope, Mr Holroyd has not merely given us a biography of Lytton Strachey, but a picture of his time as well, in particular the activities of the Bloomsbury Group. Such a canvas, however, not only demands more space, but requires that the additional area be occupied by living characters, and the more characters that are added the harder it becomes to make them come alive. And few of Mr Holroyd's attempts to depict the various young men who flitted through the gardens of Ham Spray rise above a one-dimensional level.[30]

This comment is especially applicable to the depiction of Gerald Brenan, whose personality is simply submerged beneath the weight of the archive. Who would glean for instance from Mr Holroyd's biography, that Brenan was in some ways as fine a prose writer as Strachey, his peer indeed, when he published his two classical books on Spain; and that by a delicious contradiction of character he combined an ardent interest in the mysticism of St Teresa with the appetites of a dedicated (heterosexual) sensualist? What a perfect counterpoint to the homosexual, agnostic Strachey, if the character had come alive on the page; and positioned properly in the matter of light and shade it could have been made to enlarge considerably the portrait of the main character. That Strachey himself had an eye to such dramatic possibilities is evident from his shaping of Newman's character, in his famous essay, to highlight the central figure of Cardinal Manning.

However, like Professor Ellmann, Mr Holroyd has left it to the reader to make his own selection – and there is no doubt that a journey through these massive volumes will supply the voyager with huge satisfaction as he surveys the vast swathe of information that Mr Holroyd has provided us with about Strachey and the Bloomsbury Group. But is this the satisfaction that comes from the gaining of knowledge, or the special pleasure that comes from the contemplation of a work of art? Mr Holroyd would no doubt consider the question immaterial, perhaps impertinent. But that the matter must have occurred to him at some time during the weary years of his Lytton Strachey biography's gestation, there can be no doubt, as the subject of it never himself produced a biography of more than

350 pages. The exact figures are *Eminent Victorians*: 341 pages; *Queen Victoria*: 310 pages; *Elizabeth and Essex*: 280 pages.[31]

Neither does Mr Holroyd, who writes with vigour and enthusiasm, ever indicate that he has taken any lessons from his master in the matter of style. One feels there are not many passages in his book which Lytton Strachey would have singled out for special approval. Indeed, when Mr Holroyd does leave the path of informative prose and proceeds to attempt a more ambitious approach, the effect is not always felicitous. Take these two sentences for instance from his Lytton Strachey biography (p. 889):

> Part of this activity was set up by Stephen Tomlin, who, though not as yet sucked into its circumference, spiralled around the outer rim emitting shock waves to which each of the atoms would react differently but always with an electric sensitivity.

and on page 812

> During the closing months of 1920, while Lytton was putting the finishing touches to *Queen Victoria*, the emotional *sonate à trois* that was being played between Ralph, Carrington and himself, had slowly spiralled to a *sforzando*.

One has to ask if the word 'spiralled' (difficult enough at any time to pilot through a prose passage without sacrificing balance) quite succeeds in shouldering the responsibility imposed on it of having to hold up two different metaphors in quite different contexts. But as Mr Holroyd shares with Professor Ellmann that approach which depends on a massive and indiscriminate accumulation of fact, he also shares with him a hesitancy in style when it comes to achieving the sort of prose we would seek from the biographer who would produce a work of art.

Nor, indeed, do we find any noticeable change of

approach in Mr Holroyd's *Augustus John*, published in 1974 and 1975 in two volumes.[32] With his usual energy he has amassed a vast amount of information about the life of the well-known English painter. But it is difficult to see how Augustus John's life would make a two-volume biography. Undoubtedly a painter of distinction who moved in and out of the social, literary and artistic circles of the first half of this century, and one of the founders of the New English Art Group, a friend of Joyce, Wyndham Lewis, T.S. Eliot, D.H. Lawrence and others, it is hard nevertheless to imagine that a biographer seeking to get at the kernel of his life and transmit the personality which created *Madame Suggia* and other paintings, could exceed one volume in the execution of his task. The complications of John's married life, his restless pursuit of women, his failure at a crucial moment in his career to develop his work in such a way as to place him among the major artists of the century, these are matters which when developed could form the basis of an average-sized biography.

But that they would demand two volumes to present them is an indication that Mr Holroyd has been unable to resist the temptation to use to the maximum the material available and has failed to subject himself to the discipline of choosing only that which would bring his subject alive on the page.

Professor Ellmann and Mr Holroyd clearly belong to the *bonum* school – those who would include all available facts without the use of a selective process. What then about the *pulchrum* school who will '. . . row out over that great ocean of material, and lower down into it, here and there, a little bucket . . .' – the biographer as artist as envisaged by Strachey and Maurois?

Two modern writers whom I suggest fulfil the criteria of the 'selective' school and who set out to achieve – and have achieved – a work of art in biography are Norman Mailer and Osbert Sitwell.

23

The first of these did not get off to a particularly aus-
picious beginning when he entered the biographical field
in 1965. Norman Mailer, before he published *Marilyn*,[33]
a biography of Marilyn Monroe, had already established
a substantial literary reputation with four novels, one
play and a series of essays, the most notable of these
essays being *The White Negro*,[34] a study of sociological
trends in American society which he claimed would
require a new definition of the national psyche. Mailer
had also, with *Armies of the Night*,[35] an account of his
participation in the march to the Pentagon in protest
against the Vietnam War in October 1967 (which had
been sub-titled 'History as a Novel, the Novel as History'), indicated an interest in extending parameters of
form in nonfiction writing.

He was part of a post-Second World War generation
of writers who had much influence in the fifties, and
who, through the calculated use of drugs, drink and sex,
had sought what Rimbaud termed a *'dérèglement de
tous les sens'*[36] ('derangement of the senses') in order to
free themselves from what they regarded as the calcifica-
tion of conventional existence. Fine distinctions would
later be made between the words 'hipster' and 'beatnik'
(ironically the hippies of the sixties were closer in philosophy to the beat generation than to what was strictly
the hipster stance), but nevertheless it is reasonable
enough to group Mailer along with contemporaries such
as William Burroughs, Jack Kerouac, Ginsberg, John
Clelland Holmes, even the poets Corso and Ferlinghetti,
who later would be claimed by separate schools.

There were, however, certain distinctions between
Mailer and some of the contemporaries often associated
with him. He was a Harvard graduate, who had had
an early success with a best seller *The Naked and the
Dead*,[37] based on his experiences in the Second World
War, which had made him famous overnight. But in the
maelstrom of New York in the fifties, a shared defiance

of convention often made a common bond between unlikely allies. You could wear a three-piece suit and still remain a Rimbaud at heart.

Mailer also needed to make considerable sums of money from his writing to sustain an expensive lifestyle. Not for him a cold-water flat on the lower East Side, but an apartment on Brooklyn Heights, with a floating Wagnerian interior design which looked out on the ocean. As early as 1968 he informed the author that it cost him 200,000 dollars (half a million pounds in today's money) to pay the alimony to his various ex-wives and children, before he earned a penny for himself.

In the event he developed a unique skill in extracting large advances from publishers, which distinguished him from his often penurious contemporaries. Despite this he seldom seems to have sold out. Though by his own admission he had 'twisted my nerves with benzedrine and seconal'[38] in the early fifties, he possessed the constitution and staying powers of a Mosaic Patriarch and kept his body in reasonable shape, so that when opportunities arose to involve himself in the sort of book which could bring him large capital sums, he was in a position to avail himself of them.

One such was his biography of Marilyn Monroe. A skilful entrepreneur and photographer, Laurence Schiller, had acquired a unique collection of photographs of the late Marilyn Monroe and was looking for someone to write the introduction. Mailer agreed to do this after having negotiated an advance of royalties, a considerable sum of money which he badly needed at the time. Hardly had he begun work on the introduction, however, than he became fascinated with the idea of doing a biography of her. 'I wanted to say to everyone that I know how to write about a woman.' he told *Time Magazine*. 'When I read the other biographies of Marilyn, I said to myself, "I've found her; I know who I want to write about."'[39]

The difficulty was that he wasn't prepared to do the necessary research; he proposed to use only two previous biographies of Marilyn as source material. With characteristic frankness he did some sort of deal with Fred Guiles, the author of a biography of Marilyn – *Norma Jean*.[40] He also, without making any arrangement whatsoever, stole shamelessly from Maurice Zolotow's biography of Marilyn, published in 1962.[41] To justify dispensing himself from the restraints of the biographical science, Mailer proposed to call his new work 'a novel ready to play by the rules of biography'.[42] When the book did come out it ran to one hundred thousand words. The photography was predictably excellent. But Zolotow was furious and Guiles' publisher threatened to sue (255 sections had been lifted from Guiles' book) although Mailer was able to show that he had in fact paid Guiles in advance for the right to refer to the material in his biography. He was less than fair to Zolotow whom, when it suited him, he accused of being inaccurate, but when he found some relevant material collected by him used it to prove a point on which he needed support.

There is also a whiff of a personal vendetta running through the book, with Mailer making sideswipes at Arthur Miller, the playwright who had been married to Marilyn Monroe and who like Mailer was Jewish; this led Pauline Kael the New York critic, in a *New York Times* book review, to comment that since Mailer himself had 'never been married to a famous movie queen – a sex symbol' he was furious at 'catching Miller's hand in the gentile cookie jar'.[43] Mailer as much as admitted when he was on the *Mike Wallace Show* that he was dissatisfied with what he had done. Wallace caught him on the hop by telephoning Eunice Murray, Marilyn Monroe's housekeeper, who was with her on the night of her death. It turned out that Mailer had never spoken to her though she insisted that she and

Marilyn were alone that night and that murder would
have been 'impossible'. As one of Mailer's conclusions
in the book was that Marilyn had been murdered, it was
natural enough for Wallace to ask Mailer why he had
not attempted to get in touch with Murray. His reply
was unsatisfactory:

> I hate telephone interviews. I hate that way of getting
> the facts.

When Wallace bluntly said to Mailer that it was a bad
biography because in the crucial last chapter he had
failed to do the necessary research, Mailer came clean
with disarming frankness.

> I was doing something that you don't normally do
> with a book, which is I was getting into the end of the
> book with a half-finished exploration, and I decided it
> was important enough to get out there half finished
> rather than not get into it at all.[44]

Yet, with its faults, Mailer's *Marilyn* has redeeming
qualities. The prose in places is Mailer at his best. Where
for instance has the stench of the Hollywood casting
couch risen more powerfully off the page than in this
description of the possible services Marilyn Monroe had
to render her producer Joseph Schenck in return for roles
in her early films?

> A whole part of the horror which would be in her later
> could first have come from gifts of Schenck — we never
> know which curses, evils, frights and plagues are passed
> into another under the mistaken impulse we are offering
> some exchange of passion, greed, and sexual charge.
> An old sultan with a thousand curses on his head is
> capable of smuggling anything into the mind and the
> body of a young woman — less is known about the true
> transactions of fucking than any science on earth.[45]

His theory that the linking of Robert Kennedy's name to
Marilyn's death might have been manufactured by one

of the State organizations was regarded as preposterous at the time; but in the light of what is known today, it has considerably more credibility than when it first surfaced. Within the limitations of its sources, based on two other biographies, Mailer's *Marilyn* is a good shot. It did not deserve some of the embittered shrieks it received, particularly that of George P. Elliott in *Harper's Magazine* who alleged that Mailer had turned a potential narrative marvel 'into trash' and had lost 'authority as both biographer and novelist'.[46]

What was important about his writing of *Marilyn* was that the experience he gained from it would play a large part in the genesis of a book which may be his major achievement so far. This was *The Executioner's Song*,[47] a biography of Gary Gilmore, the Texan sentenced to death for murder in Salt Lake City in the winter of 1976. Liberal organizations opposed to capital punishment in the United States, such as the National Association Against Capital Punishment and the Utah Coalition Against the Death Penalty, initiated a campaign to stop the execution. Gilmore, however, for reasons which he set out with compelling clarity, made it clear that he did not want the sentence commuted and insisted on the execution being carried out – which it was after months of legal proceedings when he was finally executed by firing squad on 17 January 1977.

Coincidentally, it was Larry Schiller, who had brought the pictures to Mailer for the Monroe book, who now put him in touch with the Gilmore project. Schiller, a former *Life Magazine* photographer, had branched out as an entrepreneur in books, movies and special magazine projects. Acting as a sort of middle man between bizarre figures of public notoriety and the media, he had picked up the rights to Susan Atkin's life in the Charles Manson case, and the last interview that Jack Ruby ever gave, in addition to interviewing Madame Nhu. But the advantage for Mailer lay in the fact that Schiller had in his possession a vast armoury of tapes, interviews, and information concerning Gilmore's background. He had hundreds of interviews with Gilmore's relatives, his prison guards, the relatives of the murdered men, and had over sixty tapes of interviews with Gilmore's girlfriend, Nicole Baker. In addition, he had acquired the rights to a set of remarkable letters Gilmore had written to Nicole from prison. As Mailer pondered on the project it seemed to him that at last he would be in a position to approach biography with a good deal of factual information instead of finding himself in the position he had been in when he started on *Marilyn*.

There also seemed in certain matters to exist an almost psychic affinity between Mailer and his subject. First there was the 'Irish' connection. For whatever reason Mailer has always believed that in his subconscious somewhere lurks an Irish alter-ego, and whether he is playing an Irish policeman in one of his own films, or being told that he has an Irish look, he will tend to attribute this apparent affinity to some early genetic inheritance.[48] Gilmore's only direct association with Ireland came through one Mary Ellen Murphy, his mother's great grandmother. But he was constantly preoccupied with this side of his ancestry, referring to 'the pull of the Emerald Isle. It's a land of magic', and among other claimed affinities, nominating as his favourite book J.P. Donleavy's classic account of Dublin in the fifties, *The Ginger Man*.[49]

Then Mailer's highly personalized religious views seemed to have found some factual expression in Gilmore's declared intention to have himself executed to pay his debt to society. In *An American Dream* (published 1965) Mailer has his chief character, Congressman Stephen Rojack, explain his late wife's arguments in favour of suicide.

... Deborah believed that if you went to Hell, you could still resist the Devil there. You see she thought there's something worse than Hell ... When the soul dies before the body. If the soul is extinguished in life, nothing passes on into Eternity when you die.[50]

Mailer told his biographer, Hilary Mills, how excited he was at finding similar concepts in Gilmore.

Maybe there is such a thing as living out a life too long, and having the soul expire before the body. And here's Gilmore with his profound belief in Karma, wishing to die, declaring that he wants to save his soul. I thought, here, finally, is the perfect character for me.[51]

Even Mailer's assessment of good and evil seems to find an uncanny echo in a passage written in one of Gilmore's letters to his lover from jail. In *An American Dream*, on page 185, Mailer has his lover Cherry say to Congressman Rojack:

I believe God is just doing His best to learn from what happens to some of us. Sometimes I think he knows less than the Devil because we are not good enough to reach Him. So that the Devil gets most of the best messages we think we're sending up.

In August 1976, the year before his execution, while his preliminary hearing was taking place, Gilmore wrote to Nicole Baker:

... I know the devil can't feel love. But I might be further from God than I am from the devil. Which is not a good thing. It seems that I know evil more intimately than I know goodness and that's not a good thing either. I want to get even, to be made even, whole, my debts paid (whatever it may take!), to have no blemish, no reason to feel guilt or fear. I hope this ain't corny, but I'd like to stand in the sight of God.[52]

Such coincidences convinced Mailer that he had at hand something he could really employ his creative energy on. He agreed that the book would run to 125,000 words and that much of the material would be based on the interviews which Schiller had already made. But Mailer couldn't have known that it would take him four years before the book was published and that in the meantime he would do over a hundred interviews himself. He found himself obsessed by the lure of fact. He flew to Utah for follow-up interviews with friends and family of Gilmore. He rented a room in Provo, Utah, for two months to get the atmosphere of the town where Gilmore had worked before he committed the murders. He even slept in the actual Holiday Inn motel room where Gilmore had spent the night of the crime, with his lover. He met Nicole Baker and was so fascinated with her that he took her to New York for a while and taught her to play chess there. He resisted all attempts to fictionalize the process — even a proposition which would have enabled him to make a film with Francis Ford Coppola. Of particular value to him was meeting with Brenda Nichol who was Gary's cousin. She had known him since she was a little child and was able to give the biographer the material for his magnificent first chapter which really brings the reader into the atmosphere of that bizarre family. Mailer went out to Oregon State to interview guards and prisoners and the warden where Gilmore had been incarcerated for many years as a younger man, and spoke to numerous convicts who were in prison with him. It is this eye-to-eye contact when talking about a third person that can kindle an image of his subject in the mind of the biographer that is impossible to come by any other way. The result was that in the end of his three years of investigation and interviewing with judges, lawyers, psychiatrists, prison guards, relatives, family and journalists, Mailer had created something which he could fairly call a 'true-life novel'. With remarkable humility he would say:

I wish I had invented it because it would have been an extraordinary piece of invention. The Literary Gods were good to me; they finally gave me a book that was asking to be written.[53]

It was of course a peach of a story with the inevitability of the classical drama, but also a vast area for exploration of the human condition. Gilmore had spent nineteen of the thirty-seven years of his life in prison and had been convicted of particularly mean and heartless crimes. But there have been few people in history who have been as sure of the moment of their death and have had at the same time as long and prolonged an opportunity for contemplating it and setting it down in words as Gilmore.

> . . . how long a journey is death? [he wrote to Nicole in his last week]. Is it instantaneous? Does it take minutes, hours, weeks? What dies first – the body of course – but then does the personality slowly dissolve? Are there different levels of death – some darker and heavier than others, some brighter and lighter, some more and some less material?[54]

A few days later he wrote:

> A simple Truth, plain, unadorned. I was never quite satisfied – I found many truths though. Courage is a Truth. Overcoming fear is a Truth. It would be too simple to say that God is truth. God is that and much, much more. I found these Truths, and others . . .[55]

On the morning of his death he told the chaplain, Fr. Meersam, that he wished to 'die with dignity'. He had been an altar boy so that when he took communion from the priest he whimsically switched roles and said 'Dominus vobiscum', while the father joining in the masquerade answered 'Et cum spiritu tuo'.[56] He was then taken out and strapped to a chair before being shot while those Utah citizens who had failed to draw lots for selection in the firing squad queued up outside in the hope of witnessing the execution.

This is one book that Mailer kept himself out of. In his earlier works of non-fiction, *Armies of the Night* and *Miami and the Siege of Chicago*,[57] he had figured prominently in the narrative. Now in proper biographical fashion he withdrew in favour of the main characters. Indeed one of the remarkable characteristics of *The Executioner's Song* is how real and well drawn are the numerous characters throughout its more than one thousand pages. He even allows us a rounded portrait of Laurence Schiller, the entrepreneur who had sold him the idea and the material in the first place. One of Schiller's virtues as Mailer has pointed out was his willingness to be interviewed himself: he 'stood for his portrait, and drew maps to his faults'.[58]

The picture Mailer draws of Schiller holed up in a Hawaii hotel, perpetually on the phone to all corners of the globe, buying, selling, packaging the material relating to a doomed man's death, is one which demonstrates that a biographical portrait if properly drawn can rival an imaginative one if only for the reason that it would be incredible if it were not supported by the stark scaffolding of fact. Perhaps the most revealing insight into the different forces that were conflicting in this strange individual's mind, is his scream into the telephone when he was being offered 125,000 dollars (which he refused) for his account of Gilmore's last minutes before he was executed: 'I'm not walking any Last Mile. I don't even know if I want the fucking guy to be executed.'[59]

Throughout the book Mailer has taken the opportunity to write minute descriptions of motel rooms, barbecues, small town coffee shops which give a *cinéma verité* effect to the picture he is creating. Whether he is writing about local lawyers, small-town businessmen, Salt Lake City police, he is always able to escape from cliché and find the human content in local life

– which cannot have been easy for someone raised in the metropolitan anonymity of America's largest city.

There is one particular scene near the end of *The Executioner's Song* which could only have occurred in the United States, and which, by the sheer authority of the facts on which it is based, acquires an impact which it undoubtedly would have lost had it been invented. This is the last-minute attempt of the Utah Coalition Against the Death Penalty and the National Association Against Capital Punishment to have Gilmore's execution commuted or postponed.

Incredibly, this began at 1 a.m. on 17 January 1977, the morning Gilmore was scheduled to be executed and when he was already preparing himself for the death he had demanded. In the early morning Judge Ritter of the District Court of the State of Utah granted a stay of execution to the Utah Coalition Against the Death Penalty on the grounds that the 'Utah death penalty has not been held constitutional by any courts'. The nearest Court of Appeal for the State Prosecutor was in Denver 500 miles away. But this did not deter these tenacious lawyers imbued with the pioneer spirit of their hardy ancestors. Up into the air they swung at 4.20 a.m. in a tiny twin-engined Kingair plane, occupied by defence lawyers, prosecutors and judges, and made for Denver, having asked the Tenth Circuit Court to convene a special sitting at 7 a.m. At 7.35 a.m. it seemed all over when the Appeal Court reversed Ritter's judgement. But no. This was the United States. The National Association Against Capital Punishment had a lawyer standing by in Washington where it was now 10.30 a.m. (Eastern Time) who managed to nobble the entire Supreme Court in their robing rooms and persuade them to hear an appeal. The Court presided over by Chief Justice Burger handed down a unanimous decision. There would be no stay. The vast area of the North American sub-continent comes into focus when one learns that though it was 10.03 a.m. in Washington, it was still only 8.03 a.m. in Salt Lake City. The Mormon tradition for punctuality would remain virtually unimpaired, and Gilmore's extermination brought on target. The surrealistic aura emanating from this extraordinary episode in some way seems related to the dull gleam of those vast Mormon Temples under whose canopies had been generated that unyielding fundamentalism which would determine Gilmore's ultimate fate. Very cleverly Mailer uses, in the third person, the thoughts of a young woman lawyer for the defence (a former Mormon) as she sits in the mountain-hopping twin-engined Kingair plane on the way to the Denver Appeal Court, to light the structure of his tale, without appearing to intrude his own personality in any way.

What made it all the more annoying to Judy [Wolbach] was the way they were seated. Judge Lewis, in order to avoid getting into, or even hearing, conversations with either side, had selected the most uncomfortable spot on the plane, a little jump seat at the back that was terribly cramped . . . Right in front of her, Hansen [the prosecutor] was asking Dorius if he had done any research on delay of execution, and there again, right in front of her, Dorius replied that the relevant cases seemed to indicate an execution was legal even if it took place after the exact hour and minute . . .

Mormonism, thought Judy, plain old primitive Christianity . . . She hated blood atonement. A perfect belief for a desert people, she thought, desperate for survival, like those old Mormons way back . . . Yessir, satisfy your bloodlust, and tell yourself you were good to the victim because blood atonement remitted the sin. You gave the fellow a chance to get to the hereafter after all . . . Primitive Christianity! She was glad she'd gone to Berkeley.[60]

One of the qualities which makes *The Executioner's Song* 'a remarkable biography' is its architectural structure. Only somebody with Mailer's combination of talents could have assembled it as he did. He had evolved an individual prose style, muscular and energetic, which he allied to a powerful imaginative insight. But biography requires specific skills. The biographer must be able to assemble his material and keep the overall picture of a vast amount of factual information in front of him as he progresses with his work. Mailer's degree in aeronautic engineering from Harvard should have assisted him in the process. Faced with one of the biggest biographical packages ever handed to a writer he was able to confront the material with structural authority. He had in fact retained an interest in engineering and had gone so far as to construct in his Brooklyn home, and keep on constant display, a futuristic city built out of Lego blocks. It was this combination of assemblage, construction, insight, atmosphere, sense of character, historical awareness and social enquiry, allied to Mailer's muscular prose style and imaginative gift that makes *The Executioner's Song* the remarkable work it is.

As soon as *The Executioner's Song* appeared with the sub-title 'true-life novel' the predictable controversy began. The argument had been going on for two decades about the relationship between non-fiction and creative writing. It had surfaced superficially with the publication of Truman Capote's *In Cold Blood*,[61] an account of the capture, trial and execution of two small-town murderers, who had slaughtered an entire family in the Middle West. Capote called his book 'a non-fiction novel' as opposed to Mailer's 'true-life novel' or his sub-title for *Armies of the Night*, 'History as a Novel, the Novel as History'.[62]

Capote has claimed in *Music for Chameleons*[63] that he invented the genre with his *The Muses are Heard*,[64] an account of the first cultural exchange to take place between the Soviet Union and the USA when a group of black Americans went to Russia to perform in *Porgy and Bess*. Capote called his report 'a short comic, "non-fiction", novel'. Later however he became more ambitious.

> I wanted to produce a journalistic novel, something on a large scale that would have the credibility of fact, the immediacy of film, the depth and freedom of prose, and the precision of poetry.[65]

This was to be *In Cold Blood*, commissioned first by William Shawn of the *New Yorker*. The trouble was that Capote hadn't reckoned with the American legal system. By the time the court appeals of the two murderers had used themselves up, it had taken seven years to get the book on the road. In the meantime, paralysed by the imminence of fact he had run out of petrol, rather like Scott Fitzgerald, driven to writing movie scripts in Hollywood. If *In Cold Blood* was a success Truman Capote stood to be a millionaire. It was a success and he did become rich. But at what a price. Kenneth Tynan thought the book a cop out: 'It seems to me that the blood in which his book is written is as cold as any in recent literature.'[66]

Read today, *In Cold Blood* doesn't stand up against Capote's best work as a first-class piece of writing. He who had admired the best stylists ('Henry James the master of the semi-colon' – 'From the point of view of the ear, Virginia Woolf never wrote a bad sentence'),[67] resorts in this 'non-fiction novel' to sentences which seem almost a parody of Zane Grey: 'When even crows seek the puny shade, and the tawny infinitude of wheatstalks bristle, blaze.'[68] Or, 'The chill of oncoming dusk shivered through the air, and though the sky was still deep blue, lengthening shadows emanated from the garden's tall chrysanthemum stalks.'[69]

He even committed the unpardonable sin in non-fiction of altering the facts to suit the end of his book, which flies in the face of Desmond MacCarthy's maxim that in biography a writer 'is an artist who is on oath'.[70] Capote invents a scene where Alvin Dewey, the Kansas State Investigator, and Susan Kidwell, Nancy Clutter's best friend, meet in a garden cemetery where the Clutters are buried close to the judge who sentenced their killers. It is a sentimental and false finish to a book which purports to be true and unsentimental. Capote admitted that he could probably have done without this last part which brings everything to rest: 'People thought I should have ended with the hangings, that awful last scene. But I felt I had to return to the town, to bring everything back full circle, to end with peace.'[71] He might have added that it was a very similar ending to that of one of his earlier and successful novels, which also came to an end in a cemetery. One revealing sentence gives us an insight into the pressures that he may have been under: 'As you may have heard,' he told a friend, 'the Supreme Court denied the appeals (this for the *third* damn time), so maybe something will soon happen one way or another. I've been disappointed so many times I hardly dare hope. But keep your fingers crossed.'[72]

Capote's characters had to die if his book was to be a success. Mailer's case was different in that his subject was already dead before he began to write the biography. But there is another important difference. Though Capote claimed to have collected over 4,000 pages of notes,[73] there is little evidence of this in his bland presentation of his main characters. It would seem in fact that he never fully grasped the implications of the biographical form, and simply wished to extend the reporting technique he had acquired in his account of the Russian tour by a company of black American performers, in *Porgy and Bess*.

I conceived of the whole adventure as a short comic 'non-fiction novel', the first.

Some years earlier, Lillian Ross had published *Picture*, her account of the making of a movie, *The Red Badge of Courage*; with its fast cuts, its flash forward and back, it was itself like a movie, and as I read it I wondered what would happen if the author let go of her hard linear straight-reporting discipline and handled her material as if it were fictional – would the book gain or lose? I decided, if the right subject came along, I'd like to give it a try: *Porgy and Bess* and Russia in the depths of winter seemed the right subject.[74]

The reference to Lillian Ross is significant. Her book *Picture*, whether creative non-fiction or not, purports to be an account of the making by John Huston of a particular film, and makes no pretence to be a biographical study.

Later Capote would reply to Mailer's description of *In Cold Blood* as a 'failure of the imagination' by implying that much of Mailer's work had come into being as a result of his own pioneering effort.

But there were those who felt differently, other writers who realized the value of my experiment and moved swiftly to put it to their own use – none more swiftly than Norman Mailer, who has made a lot of money and won a lot of prizes writing non-fiction novels (*The Armies of the Night, Of a Fire on the Moon, The Executioner's Song*) although he has always been careful never to describe them as 'non-fiction novels'.[75]

Again Capote seems to confuse the issue. *Armies of the Night* and *Of a Fire on the Moon* are narratives of actual events. *The Executioner's Song* on the other hand is a biography, an attempt to bring a personality alive against the background of the events of his life. Mailer made it clear when he wrote some years ago about the 'New Journalism' that he was in no way allying it with his venture into biography.

These days everyone is laying claim to have started the New Journalism. Truman Capote is screaming. Tom Wolfe has been writing manifestos about it for the last ten years. And Lillian Ross, who actually started it, has been silent. But I think that if I started any aspect of that New Journalism – and I did – it was that of an enormously personalized journalism in which the character of the narrator was one of the elements in the way the reader would finally assess the experience.[76]

In *The Executioner's Song* he had merely employed some of the techniques he had acquired in his early experience of non-fiction writing, and then went into an entirely new genre, that of the creative biographer, which is not to be compared with the work of Ross, Hersey or Cornelius Ryan,[77] pioneering though it may be, because they were not dealing primarily with the portrayal of personality, but with the chronicles of persons caught up in a movement of events.

The second writer whom I believe one can present as someone who had brought characters alive, through the biographical method, in such a way as to demonstrate its possibilities as an art form is Sir Osbert Sitwell. In his four volumes, *Left Hand, Right Hand!, The Scarlet Tree, Great Morning* and *Laughter in the Next Room*,[78] which he tells us quite frankly he planned 'as a work of art',[79] he has captured the essence of his time as seen through the eyes of a member of the English aristocracy. I would go so far as to say he is, if there can be such a thing, an English Marcel Proust. But it is through his portrait of his father, Sir George Sitwell, which is built up through the four volumes, that the period comes most vividly to life: and it is clear by the time he has reached the third volume that the author recognizes that the key to achieving a work of art in these chronicles is the successful recreation of his father's character and that he has concentrated all his artistic capabilities in making the portrait of his father the centre of the work. In *Laughter in the Next Room*, the fourth volume, he tells:

> At a time when people of his [father's] kind, of similar derivation, were declining in vigour and in the originality of their character [this is the English aristocracy at the turn of the century] and becoming lazy in the use of their minds, my father provided a last flash of the old fire, and summed up his own tradition – in rather the same way that, for example, Tiepolo provided the final glory, an ultimate vision, in which all the virtues and faults were emphasised, of Venetian painting. It has been my purpose to portray him – from whom I have inherited certain ranges of interest and veins of thought, but hardly ever of feeling, and against whom I so often made a counter-challenge – with the same solidity with which Boswell has caused Doctor Johnson to stand out from the shadows, with the same recognisability, so that every utterance, even the most unexpected, is immediately identifiable.[80]

But how is one to cull a few examples of the process by which Sir Osbert created his magnificent portrait, or even give a flavour of it? Perhaps a selection from the lists attached to the various boxes which Sir George kept in his upstairs rooms might give some idea of the nature of his interests and the fantastic, almost unfathomable range of his knowledge.

English Pilgrims in Tuscany in the Fourteenth
  Century
Osbert's Debts
Pig-keeping in the Thirteenth Century
My Advice on Poetry
Acorns as an Article of Medieval Diet
Lepers' Squints
Introduction of the Peacock into Western Gardens
Sweet Preserves in the Fourteenth Century

The Errors of Modern Parents
Court-life in Byzantium
The History of the Fork
The Black Death at Rotherham
Chaucer's Presumed Visit to Boccaccio.[81]

Nor was this remarkable man's energies confined to collecting the contents of these boxes. He had written an original book on the principles governing landscape gardening[82] which had become a classic and which demonstrates his own gifts as a writer of prose. The greatest part of his energy was spent in designing his various estates, either adding to the existing buildings, or recreating the landscape as a prince might have done in Renaissance Italy, damming a river to create the effect of a cascade between distant trees, 'the notes controlled by the various stones over which it fell',[83] or planning for the construction of a ruined Roman aqueduct at the end of the garden, so that a narrow arch should frame each view, or laying out two golf courses with domed pavilions, or digging a waterway which would bring his guests, in barques shaped like dragons, to tea in a Chinese pavilion erected in the leafy solitude of his woods. Before the First World War this amazing man, not content with his endless redesigning of his English estates, bought another one in Italy, between Florence and Siena – the Castle of Acciaiulo at Montegufoni which had once belonged to the Dukes of Athens. Here for the remainder of his life he was to fling himself into every sort of fantastic plan which would restore and beautify his new property. Though he would only spend some months of the year there and his restoration cost enormous sums, it was an aspect of his eccentricity that he would airily explain to acquaintances that one of the chief reasons he purchased the place was so that he would have an opportunity to make his own champagne.

Yet, despite his lavish expenditure on these indulgences of an English gentleman, Sir George had persuaded himself that he had reared a family of spendthrifts and that it was his sons, whose pocket money even after they had left school was less than a pound a week, who would bankrupt the family. Osbert was continually berated for such indulgences as going to the theatre or the ballet, or having his hair cut at Trumpers, while Sir George claimed 'he had had to exercise the strictest self-denial, giving up every pleasure in order to keep out of debt'. One of the ways he thought up to keep the bills down was to write to his youngest son's housemaster at Eton in 1915 to say he had been particularly hard hit by the war and that having read a correspondence in *The Times* on the benefits to be derived from the practice of payment in kind, he proposed to pay his son's term fees by the delivery of their value in pigs and potatoes![84]

Here let Osbert Sitwell himself present us with one of his accounts of his father's endless eccentricity:

> [He] was walking through Leicester Square, with my brother on one side of him, and with me on the other. We were both in the uniform of the Grenadiers, with large grey great-coats, and my father was wearing a top-hat and a blue heavy coat with a wide fur collar. Suddenly a bonneted Salvation Army lassie came up, and holding out a wooden money-box towards my father, jingled it, and said to him, very gently and sweetly, 'Give something for Self-Denial Week, sir!'
>
> My father stopped walking, as if overcome by the shock he had received, and then, after fixing on her for some instants a look of the utmost severity and moral disapprobation, pronounced, in patient saint-like tones, these words: 'With *Some* People, Self-Denial Week is *Every* Week.'
>
> Then he proceeded on his way.[85]

As his son points out, Sir George had learned to live with the rapidly changing ways of the Edwardian and post-War worlds simply by locking himself in an invisible suit of Gothic armour without slits for the eyes so that he saw what went on outside as he wanted to see it. He demanded that others should accede to the illusion he had created by his wearing of this mask, which he was perfectly well aware he was wearing yet which gave him a real advantage when he was dealing with other people.

And on one occasion when he was showing a group of visitors round Castle Montegufoni and had been irritated by a nervous but somewhat persistent young Englishman in the group anxious to please, he said:

'Do you see the beam up there?' . . .
'Yes, Sir George' . . .
'Well, that's very clever of you! because there isn't one . . .'[86]

It was his custom to preside over dinner at Renishaw, the Sitwell country house, like a Byzantine emperor on his throne, seated on a sofa supported by a carved and painted lion at each end, and announce to his grown-up family: 'I must ask anyone entering this house never to contradict me or differ from me in any way, as it interferes with the functioning of the gastric juices and prevents my sleeping at night.'[87]

However unlikely one may at times think some of the events and characters portrayed by Sir Osbert in his description of his father, because he is using the biographer's technique, he is always able to back it up with some corroborative evidence of a factual kind – a letter, a diary entry, a note by a contemporary, and not least by examples of the extensive correspondence which his father conducted with butlers, gardeners and estate agents which can be found in the appendices of the book. Thus the sheer impact of the facts supplied compel us to believe in the reality of the existence of his astonishing character in a way, I feel, that we might not accept, if he were to come to us through a work of fiction. In other words it has a dimension peculiar to our times. For instance could any invented description create quite the effect of a letter from Henry Moate (Sir George's butler for thirty years) to the son Osbert:

> Poor Sir George, he really is a hero for his bed. I have known him often being *tired* of laying in bed, get up to have a rest, and after he had rested get back again into bed like a martyr . . .[88]

It will surprise some perhaps that I have chosen Norman Mailer side by side with Sir Osbert Sitwell as examples of how contemporary biography has been used as an art form in our time. No two writers could be more apart in background and in their approach to the art of writing. But I think that the first has demonstrated how a creative writer can avail himself of the advances in modern technology to produce a distinctive work, and that Osbert Sitwell has shown that in setting out to write the history of his own time as an art form, he has succeeded in creating for posterity a portrait that will remain as much a part of literature as that of Leopold Bloom in *Ulysses* or the Baron de Charlus in the massive seven-volume work of Proust.[89]

2

To Tell or Not To Tell

As Virginia Woolf has pointed out, the Victorian biographer was dominated by the idea of goodness: 'Noble, upright, chaste, severe; it is thus that the Victorian worthies are presented to us.'[1] Tennyson for instance had held that Byron's affair with his half-sister Augusta Leigh, his bisexualism, his energetic promiscuity, would not have been matters for his biographer since the public had no right to know about these 'wildnesses' of Byron.[2] Tom Moore collaborated in the burning of Byron's papers by his publisher Murray, probably for honourable reasons, but can we agree that he has done posterity a service? If portraiture of real-life figures is to be an art form, was Moore not depriving us of an opportunity of some day gaining an insight into that extraordinary man's mind? Having eliminated irrefutable proof of an aspect of Byron's life, Moore then set out to do an irreproachable 'Life and Letters' with, as he wrote to his friend Hobbs, the intention of making out of it 'as good and harmless a book as I can. The public will, of course, be disappointed, but better so than wrongly gratified.'[3]

For Moore then it seems that the presentation of truth would lead to the reader being 'wrongly gratified'.

Fortunately in recent years a number of biographies of Byron have introduced us to the real person so that if the reader is 'gratified' it is because he has come in contact with the true personality of one of the great figures in European literature. Such reluctance to let the reader participate in all the information available to a biographer was prevalent until comparatively recently. When as late as 1917 Edmund Gosse wrote his life of the poet Swinburne,[4] he methodically suppressed aspects of Swinburne's life which were notorious among his friends. The consequences were disastrous. E.F. Benson, a friend of both Gosse and Swinburne, wrote:

> The result is that S. is buried – and buried by the only man who might have made him live.[5]

Gosse was quite frank in his aims in writing the biography, one of which was that he should 'try to prevent the world from ever knowing what a pig he [Swinburne] sometimes was'.[6] By his use of the word 'pig' Gosse was referring to Swinburne's sexual habits. The poet had an obsession with masochistic fantasies of a homosexual kind, not in itself a matter of startling interest, but one which there seems no good reason to withhold from the reader. The matter, however, went further. One of Swinburne's secret desires was to obtain a piece of wood from the Eton whipping block, on which he had been beaten as a boy, and on which he had witnessed the flogging of numerous unfortunate fellow pupils.[7]

But even if Gosse had decided to ignore the Eton flogging block correspondence, there was at hand when he wrote his biography an extraordinary description of Swinburne's secret life, related by Guy de Maupassant. The French writer's bizarre account was recorded by the Goncourt brothers (Jules and Edouard) in their journal after one of their famous literary dinners.

28th February 1875:

At Flaubert's, we were enthusing over the poetry of the Englishman Swinburne when Daudet exclaimed: 'Incidentally, I've heard that he's a homosexual. There are the most extraordinary stories told about his stay at Étretat last year . . .'

'Further back than that, a few years ago,' said young Maupassant, 'I saw something of him for a little while.'

'Why, yes,' said Flaubert, 'didn't you save his life?'

'Not exactly,' replied Maupassant. 'I was walking along the beach when I heard the shouts of a drowning man, and I waded into the water. But a boat had beaten me to it and had already fished him out. He had gone for a bathe dead drunk. But just as I was coming out of the water, soaked to the skin right up to the waist, another Englishman, who lived in the neighbourhood and was Swinburne's friend, came up to me and thanked me warmly.

The next day I received an invitation to lunch. It was a strange place where they lived, a sort of cottage containing some splendid pictures, with an inscription over the door which I didn't read on that occasion, and a big monkey gambolling around inside. And what a lunch! I don't know what I ate; all I can remember is that when I asked the name of some fish I was eating, my host replied with a peculiar smile that it was meat, and I could not get any more out of him! There was no wine, and we drank nothing but spirits.

The owner of the place, a certain Powell, was an English lord, according to people at Étretat, who concealed his identity under his mother's maiden name. As for Swinburne, picture a little man with a forked chin, a hydrocephalous forehead and a narrow chest, who trembled so violently that he gave his glass St Vitus's dance and talked like a madman.

One thing annoyed me straight away about that first lunch, and that was that now and then Powell would titillate his monkey, which would escape from him to rub up against the back of my neck when I bent forward to have a drink.

After lunch the two friends opened some gigantic portfolios and brought out a collection of obscene photographs, taken in Germany, all full-length and all of male subjects. I remember one, among others, of an English soldier masturbating on a pane of glass. Powell was dead drunk by this time, and kept sucking the fingers of a mummified hand which was used, I believe, as a paperweight. While he was showing me the photographs, a young servant came in, and Powell promptly closed the portfolio.

Swinburne speaks very good French. He has an immense fund of learning. That day he told us a lot of interesting things about snakes, saying that he sometimes watched them for two or three hours at a time. Then he translated some of his poems for us, putting tremendous spirit into the translation. It was very impressive. Powell is no ordinary man either; he has brought back a collection of fascinating old songs from Iceland.

The whole household, in fact, intrigued me. I accepted a second invitation to lunch. This time the monkey left me in peace; it had been hanged a few days before by the little servant, and Powell had ordered a huge block of granite to put on its tomb, with a basin hollowed out on top in which the birds could find rainwater during periods of drought. At the end of the meal they gave me a liqueur which nearly knocked me out. Taking fright I escaped to my hotel, where I slept like a log for the rest of the day.

Finally I went back there for one last visit, to find out the truth, to make certain whether or not I was dealing with perverts or homosexuals. I showed them the inscription over the door, which read: *Dolmancé Cottage*, and asked them whether they were aware that Dolmancé was the name of the hero of Sade's *Philosophie dans le Boudoir*. They answered in the affirmative. 'Then that is the sign of the house?' I asked. 'If you like,' they replied, with terrifying expressions on their faces. I had found out what I wanted to know, and I never saw them again.[8]

This description with its uncanny sense of chill is a biographer's dream. Now at one period Swinburne with his facility for turning thousands of tuneful hexameters towered over the Victorian literary scene: this despite early Republican views which he had adroitly abjured to suit his sovereign who had once murmured (perhaps encouraged by his furious polemics against the Boers in the South African war): 'I am told . . . Mr Swinburne is the best poet in my dominions.'[9] Now Queen Victoria was so naïve in matters of sex that she had refused to allow the inclusion of women in the proposed Criminal Law Amendment Act of 1891 (which criminalized sexual relations between persons of the same sex) on the grounds that such practices could not occur among females.

Is there not an irony here, worthy of comment by a biographer seeking to represent his subject against the background of his time, in the aged and virtuous Queen eulogizing the little poet of No. 2, The Pines, Wimbledon, without having the slightest idea that his sexual proclivities were of a kind which could scare the daylights out of an adept such as Guy de Maupassant? If Gosse left it out deliberately (and he should have been aware of it as the Goncourt diaries were published in 1889, and if he wasn't aware of it he hadn't done his homework), it was a dereliction of his duty as a biographer. In any event his *Life* of Swinburne appeared in 1917,[10] and in a post-Freudian atmosphere a predilection for using childhood experiences as a means of sexual arousal should not have been unnecessarily shocking to a reader, and a well arranged presentation of the facts could only have helped to make the biography less of a shambles than it turned out to be.

But Gosse was, no doubt, hampered by other considerations in his decisions whether to include such material or not. First of all, there was his own private life which left him with a degree of vulnerability. It is clear from his confessions and letters to J.A. Symonds that he had homosexual leanings.[11] Secondly he had Theodore Watts Dunton, Swinburne's boon companion and minder, and Swinburne's sister Isobel to contend with. They refused even to allow Gosse to tell the truth about Swinburne's drinking habits, which led Ezra Pound to comment: 'If he [Gosse] preferred to present Swinburne as an epileptic rather than as an intemperate drinker, we can only attribute this to his taste, a taste for kowtowing.'[12] But 'kowtowing', prurience, personal considerations should not be the concern of the modern biographer who by Virginia Woolf's standards 'whether friend or enemy, admiring or critical' had become 'an equal':

> In any case, he preserves his freedom and his right to independent judgement ... Raised upon a little eminence which his independence has made for him, he sees his subject spread about him. He chooses; he synthesizes; in short, he has ceased to be the chronicler; he has become an artist.[13]

As such the new biographer is freed from constraints which would have inhibited the writer of five decades ago. But what, if any, are the rules that a biographer seeking to create a work of art should set himself in the use of material relating to the private life of his subject? As a general principle he should deal with all aspects of his subject which tend to the 'transmission of personality'.[14] The guiding principle should be, does the material further illustrate the personality of the biographer's subject? If so it should not be left out; but neither should it be allowed to assume proportions unrelated to the central purpose of the book.

For instance, George Painter in his life of Marcel Proust dealt with the French writer's fascination for voyeurism in male brothels and in particular with his custom of hiring soldiers back from the Front to run naked round the bedroom in pursuit of live rats which they would impale with hatpins. Furthermore Proust, it was revealed, had helped furnish the brothel at 11 Rue de l'Arcade with furniture from his mother's own rooms.[15] This aspect of the personality of one of the greatest writers of the twentieth century shocked many readers who felt the material should not have been included. The image of the delicate hermit of the Boulevard Haussmann, the sad-eyed, pale-faced gentle son of a devoted mother whom readers of the massive seven-volume work had conceived as a reflection of Proust's own self, was now shattered. But if this was a false image did it not deserve such a fate? The question is do the details disclosed by the biographer enlarge our view of Proust's personality and help to bring him to life more vividly before our eyes, or do they not? The force capable of generating such fantastic rituals must have been a powerful one in Proust's subconscious, and to suppress its manifestation, however shocking or even ludicrous it might be, is to fail to convey a full portrait to the reader.

Then it has to be emphasized also that such revelations have no longer the impact they would have had fifty years ago. Television documentaries, the revolution in paperback publishing, daily and detailed reports in the newspapers of different aspects of sexual aberrations from child abuse to rape and sado-masochism, have made it acceptable to discuss openly nowadays matters which some years ago would have been confined to the 'specially reserved' sections of the British Museum.

Freud, writing as late as 1930 on the problem of creating a biography of one of his heroes, Goethe,[16] recognized that it could be necessary in order to give a rounded portrait to disclose certain unworthy aspects of a great man's character.

It is true that the biographer does not want to depose his hero, but he does want to bring him nearer to us. That means, however, reducing the distance that separates him from us: it still tends in effect towards degradation. And it is unavoidable that if we learn more about a great man's life we shall also hear of occasions on which he has in fact done no better than we, has in fact come near to us as a human being. Nevertheless, I think we may declare the efforts of biography to be legitimate. Our attitude to fathers and teachers is, after all, an ambivalent one since our reverence for them regularly conceals a component of hostile rebellion. That is a psychological fatality; it cannot be altered without forcible suppression of the truth and is bound to extend to our relations with the great men whose life histories we wish to investigate.[17]

The modern biographer could well keep that stark phrase constantly before his mind: 'forcible suppression of the truth'. He should have no truck with such tactics.

If it is accepted that the suppression of fact for reasons unconnected with the shaping of a portrait is no part of a biographer's task, it follows that to shape material to present an image which is not justified by the evidence available is equally undesirable. Earlier I have emphasized the untiring industry and sheer tenacity with which Professor Ellmann in his massive biography of James Joyce pursued every aspect of his subject's background in Dublin, including a vast number of interviews he conducted with friends or those acquainted with friends of James Joyce. But Hugh Kenner has laid the charge against Professor Ellmann that he attributes so little 'imagination' to his subject that he has allowed himself to 'borrow freely from the fictions when details are needed, secure in his confidence that if they got into Joyce's fictions they were originally facts'.[18] I came across a particular incidence of this manoeuvre when I read on page 176 of Professor Ellmann's *James Joyce*:

> But he [Joyce] delineated his difficulties in Ireland, and told of the débâcle at the tower; his father felt it confirmed his low opinion of Gogarty, whom he called 'the counterjumper's son'.

A 'counterjumper' in Dublin meant a sales assistant in a department store. Since Oliver St John Gogarty's father had been an eminent physician and what's more was the son of one, it seemed unlikely that he would ever have clerked in a department store. As I was writing Gogarty's biography at the time I explored every possible source which might reveal some evidence that his father had at some time during his medical studies in Trinity, or perhaps during some financial crisis in the family, taken even a temporary job behind the counter of a shop. But no such evidence was to be had. In fact it did not exist. What was Professor Ellmann's provenance then for this factual statement? The reference was footnote 97. When one consulted the impressive (and massive) array of sources included at the end of the book, under footnote 97 one found this brief reference: '*Ulysses*, 88(110)'.[19] On turning to page 110 of *Ulysses*[20] this is what one found:

> He cried above the clatter of the wheels. 'I won't have her bastard of a nephew ruin my son. A counterjumper's son. Selling tapes in my cousin, Peter Paul McSwiney's. Not likely!'

The 'bastard of a nephew' referred to by Simon Dedalus is Malachi Mulligan. Now undoubtedly Malachi Mulligan's character in *Ulysses* had been based on that of Oliver St John Gogarty who had lived with Joyce in the Martello Tower where the first chapter of *Ulysses* is set. But to say as Ellmann does that Gogarty's father was a clerk in a department store owned by a relative of the Joyce family, relying on the evidence in a work of fiction, reveals the potential of the sunken footnote in enabling a biographer to say virtually what he wants to in order to prove a point. Moreover, as Hugh Kenner points out, there are a number of other such 'factoids' in the biography:

> In two hundred years [Kenner writes], they will believe it happened. Never mind today's scales, we have our obligation to our posterity. Who in AD 2182 will have the patience, or the resources, to pick this cat's-cradle apart? And whoever may try it will surely be assailed for assailing something its own time judged 'definitive'.[21]

In Professor Ellmann's *Oscar Wilde*[22] one encounters somewhat similar literary legerdemain. On page 88 of the book the following appears as a footnote:

> My belief that Wilde had syphilis stems from statements made by Reginald Turner and Robert Ross, Wilde's close friends present at his death, from the certificate of the doctor in charge at that time (see p. 547), and from the fact that the 1912 edition of Ransome's book on Wilde and Harris's 1916 life (both of which Ross oversaw) give syphilis as the cause of his death.

Ellmann continues:

> That conviction is central to my conception of Wilde's character and my interpretation of many things in his later life.

It is one thing to be convinced Wilde had syphilis, but it is another to distort the evidence when it comes to stating, in order to reinforce the argument, that he died of it. If one turns to page 547 as directed by Professor Ellman, and if one inspects the medical certificate which he tells us supports the view that Wilde died of syphilis, it will be seen that there is no such reference whatsoever in the certificate.

> The undersigned doctors, having examined Mr Oscar Wilde, called Melmott, on Sunday 15 November, established that there were significant cerebral disturbances stemming from an old suppuration of the right ear, under treatment for several years.
>
> On the 27th, the symptoms became much graver. The diagnosis of encephalitic meningitis must be made without doubt. In the absence of any indication of localization, trepanning cannot be contemplated.
>
> The treatment advised is purely medicinal. Surgical intervention seems impossible.
>
> Paris, 27 November 1900   Dr Paul Cleiss
>   A 'Court Tucker MD

The reader is therefore misled by being asked to believe that a document which appears later on in the biography contains material which is not in fact included in it. Professor Ellmann, however, takes the matter even further on page 547 when he quotes from a paper, 'The Last Illness of Oscar Wilde', delivered by Dr Terence Cawthorne to the Royal Society of Medicine in 1958.[23] The quotation which Professor Ellmann uses deals with the difficulty in controlling the spread of 'otterhoea', a discharge from the ear. But since Professor Ellmann has stated his conviction, because of the doctors' certificate on Wilde's death (and from the fact that the 1912 edition of Arthur Ransome's book includes a statement by Reginald Turner, which I will deal with later), that Wilde died of syphilis, it should have been incumbent on him to give us some idea of the main thrust of Dr Cawthorne's paper. For Cawthorne had written his paper specifically to show that Wilde did not die of syphilis but of a disease of the inner ear.

> The certified cause of death [writes Dr Cawthorne] was cerebral meningitis and almost all who knew

him felt that his mode of living contributed towards his death at the early age of 46. With the exception of Frank Harris, none of his biographers who have dealt with the cause of his death have doubted that neurosyphilis was responsible for his terminal illness and that persistent alcoholic excess hastened his end.

This I do not believe, because, without wishing in any way to condone or deny his habits, I think that a careful study of his life and of his last illness must lead to the conclusion that he died of nothing less than an intracranial complication of suppurative otitis media.[24]

To have referred to Cawthorne's paper and not have disclosed that in essence it dilutes Professor Ellmann's dearly held theory is an unusual example of the use of *suppressio veri* and *suggestio falsi* in one sentence.

Professor Ellmann also makes much of Arthur Ransome's life of Oscar Wilde (published 1912)[25] and a quote which appears on page 199 of that book:

His [Wilde's] death was hurried by his inability to give up drinking to which he had become accustomed. It was directly due to meningitis, *the legacy of an attack of tertiary syphilis.* [My italics]

But a year later, in the 1913 edition, this is how the latter was worded by Ransome.

His death was hurried by his inability to give up the drinking to which he had become accustomed. It was directly due to meningitis. For some months he had increasingly painful headaches.[26]

It can be seen that Ransome, for whatever reason, had left out the reference to syphilis in the second edition. One can well imagine that a biographer, eager for material to shore up a pet theory of his, would snatch at the Ransome quote in the 1912 edition. Now it is possible that Professor Ellmann did not see the 1913 edition, but the probability is that he did because it was the one most easily available, the earlier one having been withdrawn as a result of a libel action. If he did see the 1913 edition it doesn't seem to be playing the game to have omitted reference to it. In fact it amounts to asking the reader to join in the game of hide and seek.

It has to be admitted that Strachey himself, the pioneer of 'modern biography' in the English language, was not above avoiding facts when he wished to prove a point. One of the most impressive of the four portraits in *Eminent Victorians* is that of General Gordon, in which he attempts to show that this impeccable knight-errant – in the eyes of his age *sans peur et sans reproche* – was in fact a secret drinker, in effect, what we would today call an alcoholic. Gordon in his tent at Khartoum, with the Mahdi's dervishes howling at the walls, seemingly maintaining the traditional calm of the English Raj, was not in fact displaying proconsular detachment, but, as Strachey presents it, simply the remoteness from human affairs brought on by the consumption of too much alcohol. To put it bluntly, by Strachey's account, Gordon was blind drunk most of the time.[27]

It seems, however, from recent biographies, more particularly that of Peter Johnson,[28] that Gordon was not a compulsive drinker, and that the information that Strachey had was based on rumour and without factual foundation. At least two people cited by Mr Johnson as convincing witnesses of Gordon's sobriety were alive and presumably contactable in 1915 to 1918 when Strachey wrote his famous book. Why didn't he contact them? Admittedly the personalized interview was not a technique that he used as a rule in his biography. But where corroboration was called for, and was available, someone of Strachey's scientific cast of mind should have availed himself of it. Could it be, that having formed his opinion of Gordon's alleged weakness, and finding it suitable for his overall plan or picture, he was reluctant to proceed further, lest the truth might have left him without an indispensable essay for his biography of the Victorian period?

3

Who Dares Wins

Having dealt so far with biographers who have approached their subject in the non-selective (or *bonum*) context as opposed to the *pulchrum*[1] school which seeks to present a portrait, it may be useful to look at two authors who used both approaches when they came to write biography.

The fact that Virginia Woolf and Edmund Gosse have already entered the narrative in other guises will have familiarized us with some of their views on the subject. First let us take Virginia Woolf, for it was she more than anyone else who pioneered the first major breakthrough which could provide a prototype for the new biography. Her subject was to be the novelist Vita Sackville-West, who was married to the writer and diplomat Harold Nicolson and with whom Virginia Woolf had had a passionate lesbian affair. Now Virginia Woolf wished to write a biography of her lover. So she did in her own way. When the book appeared, the *Daily Mail* greeted it with the headline: 'A Fantastic Biography: Mrs. H. Nicolson and Orlando, 300 years as Man and Woman.'[2]

Lest there might be any doubt as to who the subject of the biography was, three of the photographs in the book were of Victoria Sackville-West herself. There she was in her modern reincarnation, the gardener novelist, Lady of the Manor, looking over her farm gate at her country house, Sissinghurst, or in an earlier manifestation in court dress as supposedly painted by Sir Peter Lely. The title page of the book left no doubt as to what the author wished it to be described as. It read 'A Biography'.

But *Orlando*,[3] as Virginia Woolf called her work, is patently not a conventional biography but a revolutionary one. Starting as a sixteenth-century male Elizabethan courtier, the chief character atomizes time and space in a Bergsonian escape from the categories and, changing sex every hundred years or so with the blithe indifference of Gautier's androgynous figure, manages to live through the ages of Pope, Dryden, Swift and the Victorians, mingling with the famous characters of those periods, until finally on 11 October 1928 she crosses the narrow plank of the present, 'the cold breeze of which brushes her face', and finishes up in a Sussex mansion baring authentic female breasts to an aeroplane which hovers under moonlit clouds.

Virginia Woolf had intended writing not a biography but a novel about two women living in a house with a view of Constantinople beneath them. But as an artist should, she let her imagination carry it where it would and her fictional character began to turn into a real one. She wrote to Vita in October 1928:

> But listen: suppose *Orlando* turns out to be about Vita; and it's all about you and the lusts of your flesh and the lure of your mind . . . Shall you mind?[4]

Mind! Vita was enchanted.

> My God, Virginia, if ever I was thrilled and terrified it is at the prospect of being projected into the shape of Orlando . . . You have my full permission.[5]

In the end most of the Sackville-West, Nicolson, Woolf

circle came into the book under one guise or another. Vita's former lover, Violet Trefusis (with whom she had eloped in a romantic trans-European jaunt while their husbands followed in hot pursuit by aeroplane and train), enters into the seventeenth-century chapter in the character of Sasha, a Russian princess. Harold Nicolson, Vita's husband, who was a promiscuous homosexual in real life, features here as Captain Marmaduke Bonthrop Shelmerdine, who eventually resolves Orlando's sexual confusion by marrying her after confessing that he is not at all sure about himself in this matter:

> 'Are you positive you aren't a man?' he would ask anxiously, and she would echo, 'Can it be possible you're not a woman?' and then they must put it to the proof without more ado. For each was so surprised at the quickness of the other's sympathy, and it was to each such a revelation that a woman could be as tolerant and free-spoken as a man, and a man as strange and subtle as a woman, that they had to put the matter to the proof at once.[6]

Such surrealistic effects could only be brought off with a sure sense of prose and an artist's gift for language. There are repeated passages of great beauty throughout the book evoking the character of the different centuries in which Orlando is reincarnated.

> Troops of ruffians, men and women, unspeakably interlaced, lurched down the streets, trolling out wild songs with jewels flashing in their ears, and knives gleaming in their fists. On such a night as this the impermeable tangle of the forests on Highgate and Hampstead would be outlined, writhing in contorted intricacy against the sky. Here and there, on one of the hills which rose above London, was a stark gallows tree, with a corpse nailed to rot or parch on its cross; for danger and insecurity, lust and violence, poetry and filth swarmed over the tortuous Elizabethan highways and buzzed and stank . . .[7]

Carried on the wings of her imagination and untrammelled by an excess of fact Virginia Woolf had created a new form. But *Orlando* never made the impact that it should have. It is flawed perhaps because its author had not realized the enormity of what she had stumbled on and treated the book as something of a romp. It is a forerunner, not a final result. In March 1928 she wrote in her journal,

> I have written this book quicker than any; and it is all a joke; and yet gay and quick reading I think; a writer's holiday . . . It may fall between stools, be too long for a joke, and too frivolous for a serious book.[8]

It was E.M. Forster who discerned what he thought was a frivolous quality inherent in Virginia Woolf's work ('She stands therefore at the very entrance of that bottomless cavern of dullness: the Palace of Art')[9] and it is this lack of intellectual stamina which would have taken her beyond brilliance into genius that was responsible perhaps for the flawed nature of *Orlando*. Had she for instance taken nine years to write *Orlando* as Joyce did with his mould-breaking *Ulysses* what might have emerged? But she wasn't impressed with Joyce even if his work had had an impressive gestation period. In 1922 when the book was at the height of its fame she records in her journal that she considered the book the work of

> . . . a queasy undergraduate scratching his pimples . . . An illiterate, underbred book . . . of a self-taught working man, and we all know how distressing they are, how egotistic, insistent, raw, striking and ultimately nauseating.[10]

But Joyce had inhaled European vapours at source. Mrs Woolf in her Bloomsbury hothouse was several layers removed from that invigorating current.

Seven years later Virginia Woolf began making notes

for a biography of the art critic and artist Roger Fry who had been the lover of her sister Vanessa. In 1932 with the success of *Orlando* she had felt the siren lure of fact. 'I find myself infinitely delighting in facts for a change . . .'[11] she had written about her plans for her next book. But *Roger Fry – A Biography*[12] was not to be published until 1940, after eight years of what can only be described as a martyrdom of the pen.

As her biographer Quentin Bell has said, 'the discipline of facts bored her.' Leonard Woolf her husband was even more scathing when she showed him the draft of the book:

> It was . . . merely analysis, not history; she had chosen the wrong method, seen it from a dull angle, made even more dull by so many dead quotations.[13]

What is curious is that Virginia Woolf as a disciple of Strachey had been one of the first to lay down impeccable guidelines for the writing of 'the new biography', ones which she proved singularly incapable of putting to use herself. She who had written:

> For there is a virtue in truth; it has an almost mystic power. Like radium, it seems able to give off for ever and ever grains of energy, atoms of light . . .[14]

now sought to suppress evidence of her sister's adulterous love affair with Roger Fry. 'How,' she wrote to her sister Vanessa, 'how to deal with love so that we're not all blushing?'[15] She might have been echoing Tennyson's strictures made eighty years before about letting the world know of Byron's 'wildnesses'. Her reluctance to deal with private family matters led her to eliminate any serious discussion of Roger Fry's relationship with Helen Anrep, with whom he lived for twenty-five years before his death. In fact this is all we are told about her and, to make it worse, Virginia Woolf's able biographer, her nephew Quentin Bell, hints that his aunt by a judicious bribe to Helen Anrep bought the right to proceed as she wished.[16] Yet if Virginia Woolf wasn't prepared to take up these matters should she have taken up the writing of the book in the first place? Then we learn that Roger Fry was a close friend of both Edward Carpenter and John Addington Symonds. But there is no reference to the fact that these were both militant homosexuals who proselytized in pursuit of their predilection. Should such facts not be allowed to have their own impact?

The prose in the book is often unworthy of such a master of language and sometimes degenerates into banalities she would never have let pass in her fictional work: 'Even though he [Roger's father] inspired his children, and his daughters in particular, with profound devotion, they "always realised that there were bounds not to be overpassed".'[17] Nor can one imagine Roger Fry himself expressing pleasure at this description of his university days: 'Now Roger had become eternal as he sat talking to his friends in a Cambridge room while the moon rose and the nightingales sang.'[18] She also resorts to crude journalistic techniques to bridge gaps, as in chapter ten which deals with the Great War in a sort of *Reader's Digest* narrative, or when she uses a similar approach to describe Roger Fry's first weeks in Italy: 'Perhaps some notion of what they meant to him can best be given by making a skipping summary of their packed pages.'[19]

Leonard Woolf's judgement that she was writing against the grain was the correct one. In the last two years before publication her journals record what she was suffering.

7 July 1938: . . . sweating over minute facts. 17 August 1938: . . . abstracting with blood and sweat from the old Articles. 29 June 1939: . . . makes my head spin and I let it reel itself off. 6 September 1939: My plan is to force my brain to work on Roger.[20]

She had fallen prey to all the faults she had sought to free biography from and she suffered for it even if unconsciously. Yet she believed she had brought her friend to life in the book.

> What a curious relation is mine with Roger at this moment [she wrote in her journal after publication] – I who have given him a kind of shape after his death. Was he like that? I feel very much in his presence at the moment; as if I were intimately connected with him: . . . a child born of us. Yet he had no power to alter it. And yet for some years it will represent him.[21]

In *Orlando* she had ventured free as the wind into uncharted territory. But now under the tyranny of fact, though she believed to the contrary, her subject had died on the page.

Edmund Gosse, on the other hand, wrote two books in a sequence exactly the opposite to that of Virginia Woolf. He first wrote an unexceptional biography of his father, published in 1890, *The Life of Philip Henry Gosse FRS*,[22] and seventeen years later at the inspired suggestion of a friend created a work of art on the same subject with his *Father and Son*.[23]

The 1890 biography had the predictable limitations of the Victorian tome. It is written, we are told in the preface, 'to present a faithful picture of my father's career'. As was the fashion, incidents which might have given flashes of insight into the personality of the subject, instead of being woven into the narrative are relegated to an appendix headed 'General Characteristics'. That there are formidable dramatic possibilities for the biographer is apparent even under the dull narrative of the first biography through which Edmund Gosse takes his reader. His father's character had been shaped in the Evangelical tradition which had had such a powerful influence on Victorian England.

Philip Henry Gosse might correspond with his colleague Charles Darwin on the difference between the coo of the rock and the wood pigeon ('when we next meet I shall beg to hear the actual coo' – Darwin to Gosse, 22 September 1856)[24] but was as determined to resist the temptation of Darwin's new discoveries as a sixteenth-century Cistercian would have been reluctant to relinquish his belief in transubstantiation in the face of Lutheran heresy.

The boiling turmoil of the Victorian conscience as it wrestled with the new thought, the excitement of the awakening of that generation to the giant leaps that were being made by science, all of this can be sensed, but none of it is transmitted through the narrative style of the author. That it is in the writing somewhere there is no doubt. George Moore on the crest of his fame as a young novelist sought Gosse out at the Travellers' Club in 1882 and congratulated him on the biography; but with his eagle eye for the possibility of an imaginative work, he advised the young writer: 'A great psychological work waits to be written – your father's influence on you . . . and as a background you will have the Plymouth Brethren.'[25]

It was then with these ideas in mind germinated by George Moore that Edmund Gosse began the second book fifteen years later. Moore had stirred the artist in him. Now, as he analysed the impetus which had led him to change tack, he might, eight years before Lytton Strachey did, be laying down the principles on which a biographer should approach his subject as a work of art.

> A very great difficulty is to select [he wrote to Frederic Harrison]. My own view is that one ought to take certain vivid passages as samples or examples, elaborate them into living pictures, and entirely omit other passages of no less interest . . . [One fails if one] tries to sow with the whole sack.[26]

There is not surely a great deal of difference between his and Strachey's rowing out

> ... over that great ocean of material, and lower down into it, here and there, a little bucket, which will bring up to the light of day some characteristic specimen ...[27]

And how the figure of the father grows under this imaginative use of the facts available to present a true portrait. Here was indeed a record of a state of soul 'once not uncommon in Protestant Europe'[28] and which was about to vanish as a second major eruption was to take place in the body of Christian belief.

Strachey had conveyed brilliantly in his portrait of Cardinal Manning the battle between the Church of England and the Roman Catholic Church, the controversies of the Tractarians, the polemics of the Puseyites and the conversions of Faber and Newman, names which echo now like tinkling bells in a cloistered backgarden of Victorian propriety. But there was another side too, a furious and apoplectic Evangelicism, a religious fundamentalism into which Gosse gives us a unique insight in his description of his father, who was one of the Brethren and felt it necessary from time to time to inculcate fear into his little son of the dangers that lay outside the barque of Faith, that repelled him and his kind.

> Hand in hand we investigated the number of the Beast, which number is six hundred three score and six. Hand in hand we inspected the nations, to see whether they had the mark of Babylon in their foreheads. Hand in hand we watched the spirits of devils gathering the kings of the earth into the place which is called in the Hebrew tongue Armageddon. Our unity in these excursions was so delightful, that my Father was lulled in any suspicion he might have formed that I did not quite understand what it was all about. Nor could he have desired a pupil more docile or more ardent than I was in my flaming denunciations of the Papacy ...[29]

As a little boy, when I thought, with intense vagueness, of the Pope, I used to shut my eyes tight and clench my fists. We welcomed any social disorder, in any part of Italy, as likely to be annoying to the Papacy. If there was a custom-house officer stabbed in a fracas at Sassari, we gave loud thanks that liberty and light were breaking in upon Sardinia. If there was an unsuccessful attempt to murder the Grand Duke, we lifted up our voices to celebrate the faith and sufferings of the dear persecuted Tuscans, and the record of some apocryphal monstrosity in Naples would only reveal to us a glorious opening for Gospel energy. My Father celebrated the announcement in the newspapers of a considerable emigration from the Papal Dominions by rejoicing at 'this outcrowding of many, throughout the harlot's domain, from her sins and her plagues'.[30]

Hand in hand father and son did investigate indeed 'the number of the Beast'. But hand in hand too this eminent zoologist (Philip Gosse had made notable discoveries in his field) and his little son step through the pages of this marvellous book in pursuit of natural knowledge.

Those pools were our mirrors, in which, reflected in the dark hyaline and framed by the sleek and shining fronds of oar-weed, there used to appear the shapes of a middle-aged man and a funny little boy, equally eager, and, I almost find the presumption to say, equally well prepared for business . . . No one will see again on the shore of England what I saw in my early childhood, the submarine vision of dark rocks, speckled and starred with an infinite variety of colour, and streamed over by silken flags of royal crimson and purple.[31]

Then the dénouement is beautifully arranged when the boy, carried away in his reading of the classics by the proud gesture of Apollo, the kirtled shape of Diana, the voluminously bearded figure of Jupiter, one day asked his father to tell him about these 'Old Greek Gods'.

His answer was direct and disconcerting. He said
– how I recollect the place and time, early in the
morning, as I stood beside the window in our garish
breakfast-room – he said that the so-called gods of
the Greeks were the shadows cast by the vices of the
heathen, and reflected their infamous lives; 'it was for
such things as these that God poured down brimstone
and fire on the Cities of the Plain, and there is nothing
in the legends of these gods, or rather devils, that it is
not better for a Christian not to know'. His face blazed
white with Puritan fury as he said this – I can see him
now in my mind's eye, in his violent emotion. You might
have thought that he had himself escaped with horror
from some Hellenic hippodrome.[32]

Why is it that Gosse, who occupied a position of
power in his time (it was his influence that obtained
a Civil List grant for Joyce in 1915), should have
written but one notable book? The rest of his writings
remain unread and his critical judgement has little value
today. Desmond MacCarthy has summed it up very well:
Gosse's failure in writing the life of Swinburne was that
he heeded 'the voice of that old Dame, Discretion, to
whose warnings Mr. Gosse in writing *Father and Son*
was so fortunately deaf'.[33] It could also be said that one
reason that Gosse was 'so fortunately deaf' to 'the voice
of that old Dame, Discretion' in *Father and Son* may
have been that the book did not appear under his own
name when it was first published; and it was only seven
months later when it had been acclaimed as a masterpiece that he would acknowledge his authorship.

4

The Biographer's Way

I

We have examined the possibilities of using fact unsupported by the luxury of invented plot, as a means to achieve a work of art. We should now consider the effect in the writing of modern fiction of the use of events and characters taken directly (and without apology) from contemporary life. Two of the great novelists of this century, Joyce and Proust, both clung to fact like a drowning man might snatch at a piece of wreckage to keep him afloat.

George Painter, Proust's biographer, has recalled a conversation with the American Proustian scholar, Philip Kolb:

> What we said was everything in Proust's life is used in *A la Recherche* and everything in *A la Recherche* happened in Proust's life. That sounds axiomatic, but requires proof. I believe it's tenable and proveable.[1]

Now we do know with certainty that the infrastructure of Joyce's *Ulysses* is based on actual events which took place on 16 June 1904 and which were recorded in the Dublin newspapers on the following day.

The two works are therefore anchored in reality.

But what about the question of Proust's 'involuntary memory' as opposed to the deliberate recollection of actual events? Undoubtedly Proust regarded the process of 'involuntary memory' as of vital importance in strengthening the texture of his novel. Indeed, at one time – as his biographer George Painter has said – 'his [Proust's] first idea . . . was to write a novel which consisted entirely of the past in its pure reality as restored by unconscious memory'. But he decided to write '. . . half or more of his novel from everyday material and objective reality'.[2] The original scheme having been discarded, Proust's great novel finally became largely a *deliberate* recreation of his childhood and later life, the whole laced with a powerful stimulant provided by the 'diver' he sent down into his subconscious, to recover what he could not obtain from conscious recollection. 'A fragment of pure life', is how he has described this later process, 'preserved in its purity, which we can only know when it is so preserved, because in the moment when we live it it is not present to our memory but surrounded by sensations which suppress it.'[3]

First, there is no argument that Proust used fact as the rocklike basis for his novel. But it was obtained in two ways, one by his famous dipping of the piece of dry toast in his tea so that the memory of Auteuil-Combray came rushing back to him, or the other by the more orthodox racking of his memory to give him the basis for his narrative and creation of character. But to say, as Beckett does, that the whole of Proust's world comes out of a teacup, and not merely Combray and his childhood, is untenable.[4] As Painter points out, Proust eventually quite rightly decided to write half or more of his novel from everyday material and objective reality.[5]

Joyce's procedure is remarkably similar. His 'involuntary memory' (though he would not have called it that), manifests itself in the interior monologue which tells us so much about the workings of the minds of Stephen Dedalus and Leopold Bloom. As he walked 'into eternity along Sandymount Strand'[6] the smell and sound could have engendered in him a similar response to that of Proust when he had Marcel hear the Vinteuil sonata,[7] tasted himself the madeleine,[8] or experienced his notorious stumble.[9] However, when he comes to record what actually happened, Joyce hangs on with limpetlike tenacity to the buttressing support of fact. His novel is virtually without plot, but the events in it are tightly interwoven with those which occurred on two days as recorded in the newspapers of 16 June 1904. Real characters appear in the book under their actual names, John Eglington, Richard Best, Reuben Dodd, Fr. Conmee SJ, John O'Connell, amongst others.

Here are some of the events in *Ulysses* relating to the events of 16 June 1904 as recorded in the *Freeman's Journal*, the *Irish Independent* and the *Evening Telegraph*.

On page 333 of *Ulysses* we learn of how Throwaway's win in the Ascot Gold Cup at 20−1 causes embarrassment for Leopold Bloom who is wrongly suspected of 'having a few bob on Throwaway' and going away 'to gather in the shekels'. Here is the list of runners for that day as reported in the *Freeman's Journal*:

		age	st.	lb.
M.J. de Bremond's Maximum II	In France	5	9	4
Mr. W. Bass's Sceptre	A. Taylor	5	9	1
Lord Ellesmere's Kroonstad	J. Dawson	4	9	0
Lord Howard de Walden's Zinfandel	Beatty	4	9	0
Sir J. Miller's Rock Sand	Blackwell	4	9	0
Mr. W. Hall Walker's Jean's Folly	Robinson	3	7	4
`Mr. F. Alexander's Throwaway*	Braime	5	9	4
M.E. de Blaskovits's Beregvolgy	In France	4	9	0
Count H. de Pourtales's Ex Voto	In France	4	9	0

Count H. de Pourtales's Hebron II	In France	4	9	0
M.J. de Soukozznotte's Torqusto Tasso	In France	4	9	0
Mr. Richard Croker's Clonmell	In Ireland	3	7	7

It will be noted that Throwaway is number six in the list and he is rated as an outsider at top weight. In the *Evening Telegraph* of that day we learn that Throwaway 'romped home in a canter'.

On page 235 of *Ulysses* we find Leopold Bloom noting:

> An elderly female, no more young, left the building of the courts of chancery, king's bench, exchequer and common pleas, having heard in the lord chancellor's court the case in lunacy of Potterton, in the admiralty division the summons, ex parte motion.

The legal diary of 16 June in the *Freeman's Journal* has this under 'Law Notices in the High Court of Chancery'. It will be noted that the last name is Potterton.[10]

> Lord Chancellor – In Lunacy – Before the Registrar – 11.30 o'clock – Courtenay, of unsound mind, ex parte; Plunkett, do., adj. summons; Logan, do., summons; Moorhead, do., do.; Howlett, do., do.; Gattey, do., do.; Martin, do., do.; Potterton, do., do.; Jeffares, do. adj. statement; Dumon, do., settle report; St. George, do., discharge queries; Chapman, do., vouch account; Keating, do., do.; Potterton, do., do.

(One wonders how Joyce, usually so meticulous in such matters, confused the Admiralty Division with the Chancery Court.) In 'Hades', page 93, Bloom ponders on whether or not he will go to see Mrs Bandman Palmer in the play *Leah*, that night in the Gaiety Theatre. In the amusements section of the *Freeman's Journal* this appears:

GAIETY THEATRE

MRS. BANDMANN-PALMER

Supported by her specially selected London Company

THIS EVENING (THURSDAY) AT 8

LEAH

Tomorrow (Friday) – Mary Queen of Scots
Saturday evening – Jane Shore
Usual prices: Box office at Cramer's and evenings at
Theatre, also at Shelbourne Hotel (for balcony stalls
and boxes).
Next week – Mr. Charles R. Stone's Famous Musical
Comedy Co.
Latest and greatest American Success

WHAT BECAME OF MRS. RACKETT

Turning to the sports page again we find that H.V.
Thrift has made 16 not out playing cricket for Trinity
College against the County Kildare team during Trinity
week. Next day he will be the hot favourite in a race
which will be reported in the *Freeman* the following
morning, a quarter-mile flat handicap in which he would
take second place. Joyce records the starters in this race
word for word on page 253 of *Ulysses*, even spelling
correctly the unusual name Morphy, when he could
easily have taken it for a printer's error for the name
Murphy.

Thither of the wall the quartermile flat handicappers,
M.C. Green, H. Thrift, T.M. Patey, C. Scaife, J.B.
Jeffs, G.N. Morphy, F. Stevenson, C. Adderly and W.C.
Huggard started in pursuit.'

Names of Irish people who have left property in
England and died or got married there are reported in

the *Irish Independent* of 17 June 1904. These are the ones the Citizen refers to in the Cyclops scene:

> Look at this, says he. *The Irish Independent*, if you please, founded by Parnell to be the workingman's friend. Listen to the births and deaths in the *Irish all for Ireland Independent* and I'll thank you and the marriages.
>
> And he starts reading them out:
>
> – Gordon, Barnfield Crescent, Exeter; Redmayne of Iffley, Saint Anne's on Sea, the wife of William T. Redmayne, of a son. How's that, eh?[11]

Joyce was never above using his writings to work off old scores and *Ulysses* has many oblique references to those who he considered had caused harm to himself or his family. For instance Reuben Dodd, a Dublin moneylender, had in the course of his business to evict the Joyce family from various dwellings on different occasions. Joyce puts Reuben and his son into the novel on page 96. They appear in an anecdote related in the Hades scene as the mourners proceed to Paddy Dignam's funeral in Glasnevin.

> Martin Cunningham thwarted his speech rudely.
>
> – Reuben J. and the son were piking it down the quay next the river on their way to the isle of Man boat and the young chiseller suddenly got loose and over the wall with him into the Liffey.
>
> – For God's sake! Mr Dedalus exclaimed in fright. Is he dead?
>
> – Dead! Martin Cunningham cried. Not he! A boatman got a pole and fished him out by the slack of the breeches and he was landed up to the father on the quay. More dead than alive. Half the town was there.
>
> – Yes, Mr Bloom said. But the funny part is . . .
>
> – And Reuben J., Martin Cunningham said, gave the boatman a florin for saving his son's life.
>
> – A stifled sigh came from under Mr Power's hand.

>   – O, he did. Martin Cunningham affirmed. Like a
> hero. A silver florin.
>   – Isn't it awfully good? Mr Bloom said eagerly.
>   – One and eightpence too much, Mr Dedalus said
> drily.'

This was based on a good Dublin yarn which probably had its origins in a report in the *Irish Worker* of 2 December 1911, published by Jim Larkin, the Labour leader. Even the witty dénouement in the *Ulysses* extract derives from a Larkin comment: 'Mr. Dodd', wrote Larkin, 'thinks his son is worth half-a-crown. We wouldn't give that amount for a whole family of Dodds.'[12]

In May 1958 Reuben Dodd Junior was trying to get the racing results on the BBC when he accidentally switched on the Third Programme. There to his astonishment he heard his own name mentioned and not at all in a pleasant context. He commenced an action for defamation against the BBC which was settled with an apology and damages for the plaintiff.[13]

That Joyce must have scoured the *Freeman's Journal* of 16 June 1904 with his magnifying glass is indicated by this tiny extract from the small print of the Shipping News for that day. Under the heading 'Dublin Shipping List yesterday – Coastwise arrival', we find '*Rosevean* from Bridgewater with bricks'. On page 545 of *Ulysses* in the Cab Shelter scene we find the sailor telling Stephen and Leopold: 'We come up this morning eleven o'clock. The threemaster *Rosevean* from Bridgwater with bricks. I shipped to get over. Paid off this afternoon. There's my discharge. See? W.B. Murphy, A.B.S.'

Indeed that he attached an almost superstitious importance to facts in his novel is shown from the well-known letter that he wrote to his Aunt Josephine in November 1921[14] asking her if it were possible for an ordinary person to climb over the railings of No.

7 Eccles Street either from the path or the steps, lower himself from the lowest part of the railings till his feet were within two or three feet from the ground and drop unhurt. It will be recalled that 7 Eccles Street was Leopold Bloom's house and that he and Stephen Dedalus were attempting to get into the house by this means early on 17 June 1904. It is not surprising then to find in the same letter a question about the cold weather of February 1893 and whether the canal was frozen or not, or to learn later that Joyce wanted to know the exact number of steps leading into the Jesuit Church in Gardiner Street. So many massive tables of facts are unleashed on the pages of *Ulysses* that it is almost as if Joyce is seeking to impose on his reader the necessity of adverting to the banal, so as to discover the importance of what actually is, as opposed to what is imagined, and in this way achieve a novel synthesis. By abandoning plot in the accepted sense of the word Joyce elevated the status of the factual – and it has been suggested in the process may have finished the novel in its current form by making it increasingly difficult for the writers coming after him to write in traditional modes.

The fact that I myself, born twenty-five years after the year in which *Ulysses* is set, had a personal acquaintance with at least four of the people who appear under their own names in *Ulysses* is an indication of how determined Joyce was to depict real persons and actual events in Ulysses.

I acted as a barrister for Reuben Dodd in his defamation case against the BBC, and was much impressed with him. He was a dear old man who had a solicitor's office of the Dickensian kind on the Dublin Quays in which as far as I could see reposed only three books: *The Compleat Angler* by Isaak Walton, *The Solicitor's Year Book for 1924* and *The Racing Calendar* for the current year. Dodd had been at Belvedere with Joyce, to whom he had taken a dislike, he told me, because as an altar boy he alleged 'Jimmy' used to steal the altar wine.

Another real-life person I knew who appears in *Ulysses* was Richard Best, the scholar and librarian who comes into the library when the discussion on Hamlet takes place: '. . . a blond ephebe. Tame essence of Wilde.' ' . . . beautifulinsadness Best . . .'

I used to take delicious afternoon teas with Best, who was full of rollicking yarns of Synge, George Moore and Oscar Wilde, and who as he would escort me to the door would inevitably confide as a parting shot that he had burnt in 1909 all Joyce's letters to him, as he decided he 'would come to no good'. It was his custom also to deny his constant over-use of the phrase 'don't you know', as attributed to him in *Ulysses*, and then somewhat weaken his contention by adding absentmindedly as he would say goodbye, 'don't you know'.

H.V. (Harry) Thrift does not perhaps qualify as a character in *Ulysses*. But he is included in the list of runners at the starting line in the race that Leopold Bloom reads about outside the railings of Trinity College Park on 16 June 1904, and his 16 not out for the College side against County Kildare is also recorded in the book. He recently achieved notoriety by having his name edited from *Ulysses: The Corrected Text* by Professor Hans Walter Gabler of the University of Munich (1986) and replaced by 'H. Shrift'. It is now however generally accepted that Professor Gabler's computer erred and we can freely admit H.W. Thrift once more to the pantheon of *Ulysses*.

Harry Thrift lived across from my house in Highfield Road, Rathgar, and I would therefore see him almost every morning after he had become vice-provost of Trinity. A distinguished mathematician and a fellow of the college, he had made his mark early as an international rugby footballer and athlete of repute. My most vivid recollection of him is seeing him crouched with eagle eye at the finishing post at the College Races, his finger poised on the stop watch which he would press as the tape was broken, before rising choleric-faced and infallible to announce the result.

In the natural order of things I came to know Oliver St John Gogarty (Malachi St Jesus Mulligan), as I was his biographer. I would hear him recite with suitable solemnity his 'The Ballad of Joking Jesus' which Joyce lifted *en bloc* from a letter written to him by a friend of Gogarty's, Vincent Cosgrave, in 1907, and inserted in *Ulysses*. Gogarty also told me the origin of the 'joyous dactyls' which Joyce gives to the 'Buck' in *Ulysses*. 'Malachi Mulligan, two dactyls ... Tripping and sunny like the buck himself.' (Penguin edition of *Ulysses*, page 10.)

As Gogarty related it, Moore had given the name Oliver Gogarty to a character in his novel *The Lake*, a renegade priest who runs away with the local school-mistress. When Gogarty's mother, understandably annoyed, went round to Moore's house to complain, Moore greeted her with: 'Madame, supply me with two such joyous dactyls and I will gladly change my name.' It was Joyce who eventually, with his acute ear, discovered the dactylic equivalent.

Though I did know these four, on a personal level, it should be remembered that Joyce's period was two generations removed from mine. It can be imagined then how many other 'real' persons in *Ulysses* would have been familiar to Joyce's own generation.

It was no accident that Joyce chose to make use of so many characters who had an actual existence of their own and to insert real events into *Ulysses*. He recognized the primacy of the factual, in a society obsessed with self-inquisition, and daringly, almost with disdain, showed how, set in the mosaic of a work of art, it can illumine the final result.

II

But while these two works which were to break the mould of the novel were in gestation, another writer had published a work of biography which he would later claim anticipated both Joyce and Proust.

In later years, sitting in front of his fire at 121 Ebury Street, London, with his Aubusson carpet on the floor and his Manet painting on the wall, George Moore would throw out his hands in a gesture of helplessness and self-deprecation and assert that his *Confessions of a Young Man* had inspired Joyce's *A Portrait of the Artist as a Young Man*, while his *Hail and Farewell* was the model for Proust's *A la Recherche du Temps Perdu*.[1]

Certainly Moore's record as an innovator is impressive. He had introduced the realism of the French school with his novel *A Mummer's Wife*[2] and had popularized the works of the Impressionist painters with his brilliant essays on Manet, Degas and others who had been his friends in Paris.[3] His essay on Verlaine in *The Contemporary Review* had virtually introduced that poet to English readers.[4] As well, Joyce had certainly borrowed from Moore's novel *Vain Fortune*[5] for 'The Dead' in his book of short stories, *Dubliners*,[6] and more than likely conceived the form that collection took after reading Moore's *The Untilled Field*.[7]

A strong track record indeed, though far from conclusive proof that Moore had succeeded in influencing Proust and Joyce in the way he claimed. Nevertheless, in *Hail and Farewell* there is evidence that with his customary prescience for what was new in art, Moore has laid down impressive guidelines for the blend of fact and imaginative recreation that the new biography might encompass. The genesis of *Hail and Farewell* came from Moore's return from London to Dublin at the height of his fame in 1901. He had come to believe that the English language had become 'a worn-out defaced coin . . . a language of commerce',[8] and was convinced that a renaissance was about to take place in Ireland in which he intended to take part. Artists, however, are steered by forces that they wot not of, and what he had hoped for from his return didn't materialize. He never succeeded in assimilating himself into the Dublin literary scene which was buzzing at the time like a beehive with chatter and industry; but as an outsider looking on, and collecting information through his famous literary evenings, he got the material for his finest book which he based on his literary experience in Dublin, and having published it, returned to London, there to be regarded as a Grand Old Man of Letters till his death in 1933.

In the preface to *Hail and Farewell* he makes the claim that nature provides better plots than fiction writers can.

> A novel is the story of a man's life, and I think we shall find that Nature provides ends for lives more strangely significant than any invented by story-tellers. The end of Beau Brummel at Nice seems to me one of Nature's triumphs; in it she has surpassed anything that I remember for the moment in Tolstoy, or Turgenev, or Tchekov or Balzac.[9]

Moore also considered that Nature had invented an end for Napoleon's life that equalled the one she achieved for Beau Brummell. As for Tolstoy:

> . . . Nature, having watched the preacher all the while, decreed an end the significance of which cannot escape even the most casual reader: a flight from his wife and home in his eighty-second year, and his death in the waiting-room of a wayside railway station in the early hours of a March morning.[10]

Moore then tells us that Nature has underwritten the entire composition of his own latest book:

> . . . every episode and every character was a gift from Nature, even the subject itself.[11]

He is not afraid to see himself as a recorder because he sees no difference between the artist in this mode and the recorder. He is Proust without the madeleine, one who is prepared to rely on the summoned image for his art rather than await the involuntary one, but at the same time (perhaps believing plot is exhausted) prepared to use the actual events of the day as if they were unfolding like the narrative of a novel.

> Highly favoured am I among authors! rose to my lips instinctively, I might say incontinently, as I opened my garden gate one morning in May, for the true significance of the words was not perceived by me whilst I worked at Nature's bidding, taking down her many surprising inventions, thinking they were my own because they happened to come my way. For Nature is a sly puss; she sets us working, but we know nothing of her designs; and for years I believed myself to be the author of *Hail and Farewell*, whereas I was nothing more than the secretary . . .[12]

So it is as a secretary of Nature that he takes on a work of biographical narrative stretching into three volumes and containing at least three major portraits besides many minor ones, all held together by his own narrative as he perambulates through Dublin during those years that he lived there from 1901 to 1912.

The three full portraits are of W.B. Yeats, Edward Martyn and George Russell: and there are as well a number of side sketches. By exquisite arrangement of the narrative Moore has managed to imbue his book with the sense of romance that he attributes to the lives of the three exemplars Brummell, Napoleon and Tolstoy quoted in his introduction.[13]

Edward Martyn, a celibate Wagnerite landlord, who founded the Irish Literary Theatre with Yeats and Lady Gregory, is really only known (albeit unfairly) through Moore's wonderful portrait of him, and George Russell, or AE as he was known, has again somewhat unfairly been relegated to the perimeter of the Irish literary giants of the period. But Yeats is an internationally recognized figure and there is a yardstick therefore available against which to match him. The introduction of Yeats's character is beautifully established as the poet comes to London with Edward Martyn, to see the great man of letters about the founding of an Irish Theatre in Dublin. Moore, seated in his rooms in the Temple, sees Martyn (who was his cousin) side by side with Yeats as:

> ... great in girth as an owl (he is nearly as neckless), blinking behind his glasses, and Yeats lank as a rook, a-dream in black silhouette on the flowered wall-paper ...
> It is Yeats, I said, who has persuaded dear Edward, and looking from one to the other, I thought how the cunning rook had enticed the profound owl from his belfry — an owl that has stayed out too late, and is nervous lest he should not be able to find his way back; perplexed, too, by other considerations, lest the Dean and Chapter, having heard of the strange company he is keeping, may have, during his absence, bricked up the entrance to his roost.
> As I was thinking these things, Yeats tilted his chair in such dangerous fashion that I had to ask him to desist, and I was sorry to have to do that, so much like a rook did he seem when the chair was on its hind legs.'[14]

This sets up the style of the portrait, a mixture of satire, deprecation, high comedy and shrewd analysis, but beneath it all there is the recognition of Yeats as a man of genius, which is maintained throughout the book.

At one stage Moore claims to have experienced in

Yeats's presence the same transcendental uplift he had received from a Brahmin many years before.

> . . . now by the side of the lake [Coole Lake], hearing Yeats explain the meaning of his metaphysical pirate afloat on Northern waters, it seemed to me that I was listening again to my Indian. Again I found myself raised above the earth into the clouds; once more the light was playing round me, lambent light like rays, crossing and recrossing, waxing and waning, until I cried out, I'm breathing too fine air for my lungs. Let me go back. And, sitting down on a rock, I began to talk of the fish in the lake, asking Yeats if the autumn weather were not beautiful, saying anything that came into my head, for his thoughts were whirling too rapidly and a moment was required for me to recover from a mental dizziness.[15]

When Yeats got into full flight of conversation the myths of ancient Ireland began to take life beyond Moore's eyes.

> . . . whereas Yeats and his style were the same thing; and his strange old-world appearance and his chanting voice enabled me to identify him with the stories he told me, and so completely that I could not do otherwise than believe that Angus, Étaine, Diarmuid, Deirdre, and the rest, were speaking through him. 'He is a lyre in their hands; they whisper through him as the wind through the original forest; but we are plantations, and came from England in the seventeenth century. There is more race in him than in anyone I have seen for a long while,' I muttered, while wending my way down the long stairs, across Fountain Court, through Pump Court, by the Temple Church, under the archway into King's Bench Walk.[16]

But Moore's mischievous eye is constantly alert. He sees Yeats at the edge of Coole Lake:

> . . . looking himself in his old cloak like a huge umbrella left behind by some picnic party.[17]

And there is the extraordinary episode during the first week of *The Countess Cathleen*[18] in the Antient Concert Rooms in Dublin in which Yeats figures almost as a character out of the Commedia dell' Arte.

His play seemed to be going quite well, but in the middle of the last act some people came on the stage whom I did not recognise as part of the cast, and immediately the hall was filled with a strange wailing, intermingled with screams; and now, being really frightened, I scrambled over the benches, and laying my hand upon Yeats's shoulder begged him to tell me what was happening. He answered, The *caoine* – the *caoine*. A true *caoine* and its singers had been brought from Galway. From Galway! I exclaimed. You miserable man! and you promised me that the play should be performed as it was rehearsed. Instead of attending to your business you have been wandering about from cabin to cabin, seeking these women. Immediately afterwards the gallery began to howl, and that night the Antient Concert Rooms reminded me of a cats' and a dogs' home suddenly merged into one. You see what you have brought upon yourself, miserable man! I cried in Yeats's ear. It is not, he said, the *caoine* they are howling at, but the play itself.[19]

Yeats must have been furious at Moore's account of a speech he gave to raise funds for Hugh Lane's Gallery of Modern Art but despite Moore's comic distortion, it is a marvellous piece of descriptive prose and stands on its own merits.

Yeats, who had lately returned to us from the States with a paunch, a huge stride, and an immense fur overcoat, rose to speak. We were surprised at the change in his appearance, and could hardly believe our ears when, instead of talking to us as he used to do about the old stories come down from generation to generation he began to thunder like Ben Tillett against the middle classes, stamping his feet, working himself into a great temper, and all because the middle classes did not dip their hands into their pockets and give Lane the money he wanted for his exhibition. When he spoke the words, the middle classes, one would have thought that he was speaking against a personal foe, and we looked round asking each other with our eyes where on earth our Willie Yeats had picked up the strange belief that none but titled and carriage-folk could appreciate pictures. And we asked ourselves why our Willie Yeats should feel himself called upon to denounce his own class: millers and shipowners on one side, and on the other a portrait-painter of distinction; and we laughed, remembering AE's story, that one day whilst Yeats was crooning over his fire Yeats had said that if he had his rights he would be Duke of Ormonde. AE's answer was: I am afraid, Willie, you are overlooking your father – a detestable remark to make to a poet in search of an ancestry; and the addition: We both belong to the lower-middle classes, was in equally bad taste. AE knew that there were spoons in the Yeats family bearing the Butler crest, just as there are portraits in my family of Sir Thomas More, and he should have remembered that certain passages in *The Countess Cathleen* are clearly derivative from the spoons.[20]

Yet the artist in Moore would always see to it that Yeats's true stature raised itself above the often ludicrous situations he placed him in.

She [Lady Gregory] never would have written a play if she had not met Yeats, nor would Synge, who is now looked upon as an artist as great as Donatello or Benvenuto Cellini, and perhaps I should not have gone to Ireland if I had not met Yeats; and if I had not gone to Ireland I should not have written *The Lake* or *The Untilled Field* or the book I am now writing.

So all the Irish movement rose out of Yeats and returns to Yeats. He wrote beautiful lyrics and narrative poems from twenty till five-and-thirty, and then he began to feel that his mission was to give a literature to Ireland that should be neither Hebrew, nor Greek, nor French, nor German, nor English – a literature

that should be like herself, that should wear her own
face and speak with her own voice, and this he could
do only in a theatre. We have all wanted repertory
theatres and art theatres and literary theatres, but these
words are vain words and mean nothing. Yeats knew
exactly what he wanted; he wanted a folk theatre, for
if Ireland were ever to produce any literature he knew
that it would have to begin in folk, and he has his
reward. Ireland speaks for the first time in literature in
the Abbey Theatre.[21]

This splendid biographical portrait of Yeats against
the background of the Irish Literary Renaissance, is in
sharp contrast to Yeats's own attempts to deal with
Moore's personality in his own memoirs *Dramatis
Personae*. Allowing his dislike for Moore to overwhelm
him, Yeats descends to caricature. Sneering at Moore's
ancestry and social background was a shabby stratagem
for the son of Sligo merchants, especially since Moore's
people were in fact landed gentry with a long pedigree.

> Moore's grandfather [Yeats wrote] or great-grandfather
> had been a convert, but there were Catholic marriages.
> Catholic families, beaten down by the Penal Laws, des-
> pised by Irish Protestants, by the few English Catholics
> they met, had but little choice as to where they
> picked their brides; boys, on one side of old family,
> grew up squireens, half-sirs, peasants who had lost
> their tradition, gentlemen who had lost theirs. Lady
> Gregory once told me what marriage coarsened the
> Moore blood, but I have forgotten.[22]

The 'I have forgotten' is a master touch. Yeats of
course had not forgotten but rather than risk a possible
challenge to the accuracy of his statement he chose to
consign it to some limbo where it could be difficult
to check against fact. In another section of *Dramatis
Personae* he manages to cast Moore in such a ludicrous
light that it is hard to believe the anecdote had any real
basis in fact.

In the early autumn Zola died, asphyxiated by a charcoal stove. Innumerable paragraphs and leading articles made Moore jealous and angry; he hated his own past in Zola. He talked much to his friends on Saturday nights. 'Anybody can get himself asphyxiated.' Then after some six weeks announced that he himself had awakened that very morning to smell gas, a few minutes more and he would have been dead; the obsession was over.[23]

Yeats however let himself down completely when he denies Moore the one gift that was undoubtedly his, that of an artist in words and a master of prose.

[Moore] had gone to Paris straight from his father's racing stables, from a house where there was no culture, as Symons and I understood that word, acquired copious inaccurate French, sat among art students, young writers about to become famous, in some café; a man carved out of a turnip, looking out of astonished eyes. I see him as that circle saw him, for I have in memory Manet's caricature. He spoke badly and much in a foreign tongue, read nothing, and was never to attain the discipline of style ... he was Milton's lion rising up, pawing out of the earth, but, unlike that lion, stuck half-way.[24]

This is little short of preposterous. What Yeats calls 'Manet's caricature' hangs in the Metropolitan Museum in New York today, Le noyé repêché,[25] and is held by some to be the painter's best portrait. As to never attaining 'to the discipline of style': whether as a realist or in later years a writer in the symbolist manner, Moore's prose style was universally acclaimed and would lead Charles Morgan later on to make the somewhat audacious claim that Moore had 'twice re-created the English novel'.[26]

Wily old fox that he was, Yeats induced Lady Gregory to take an action for defamation against Moore when *Hail and Farewell* appeared in serial form in 1912, but waited himself until his protagonist was dead before he unloaded his fireballs on him.

It was T.S. Eliot who first discerned Yeats's inability to keep himself out of the portraits he drew for his memoirs, when he commented in a review of *The Cutting of an Agate* which appeared in the *Atheneum* (July 1919) that 'The weakness of his [Yeats's] prose is similar to that of his verse. The trouble is not that it is inconsistent, illogical or incoherent, but that the objects upon which it is directed are not fixed; as in his portraits of Synge and several other Irishmen, we do not seem to get the men themselves before us, but feelings of Mr Yeats projected.' Biography requires what Moore possessed in abundance, the long hard accumulation of fact, the sifting through of information, the gradual emergence of character and then the final touch to catch the character in the net of prose. Yeats lacked this quality and the result is apparent in his often cruel caricatures of some of the characters who appear in his memoirs, however amusing they may be.

5

Personal Record

Having discussed the problems facing the modern biographer, I think it might not be inappropriate to discuss those which I myself encountered from time to time in attempts to confront questions which I have raised here.

As I said, between the two approaches, that of the chronicler and that of the biographer as artist, I am an unrepentant Stracheyite. I do believe that Strachey may have been at fault at times in refusing to relinquish the lofty height of his biographer's perch and not to have sought more interviews from those who may have known his subjects. But his method to 'select', to relieve his reader of the burden of useless material and retain only that which illuminated the character or period he was writing about, seems to me indubitably to be the right one.

One has of course at the commencement of each biography to collect the facts – and frequently there are mountains of them. Then the first temptation has to be resisted, that of the domination of the filing cabinet. How often after months of research had one uncovered a piece of information or arrived at a conclusion that however fascinating in itself would not only fail to contribute to the final portrait but would distract from it. It had to be cast aside. The second temptation was to rush to impose a scheme or form on the accumulated facts. Form should emerge from the facts, of its own volition. It has its own dynamic. When it is beginning to take shape in the mind then one may presume to erect a scaffolding, so to speak. But this scaffolding is only the structure on which to build and as the character is fleshed out less and less of the structure will remain, until finally the personality of the subject will have been caught up and the framework becomes unnecessary. The oil paint, so to speak, will have replaced the original pencil lines.

Anyone who has watched a sculptor mould the head of a sitter will have an idea of how the biographer who hopes to give the true portrait of his subject should work. Picture the sculptor faced with the amorphous mass of clay on his stand in front of him; as his fingers touch the clay, they begin to dance athletically, snatching a piece here, putting another piece there, all the time his eyes alight with that particular glow characteristic of imaginative activity, till finally from the inert mass before him something approaching the likeness which he is seeking to create will begin to emerge. So, too, the biographer. He must play with his material, turning it this way and that, standing back to look at it in one light then another, then seizing swiftly the image that he glimpses lest it should vanish and be difficult of recovery, and finally transferring his finished portrait to the printed page where it must meet the infallible test of the reader's eye.

Often he will get little credit for launching himself on the perilous seas of intuition. He will be blamed for ignoring this aspect, overemphasizing that. But he stands or falls by the energy and integrity of his portrait in so far as it has a life of its own and is the one he has chosen to portray. Nor, alas, as one progresses, and as one biography follows another, does the process become less difficult.

In a recent work, *Celtic Dawn*, I found myself up against an impasse that had to be resolved before I could get even into first gear. I had been commissioned to write a book about the writers of what is known now as the Irish Literary Renaissance. I started off cheerfully enough doing a number of conventional draft portraits of figures of the time, hoping that they would give me some inkling of how I would finally shape the work. But as I got deeper and deeper into my subject the more I began to despair of ever finishing it. It eventually was to take me six years.

What I found myself engaged in now was the biography of a period. One knew of course Walter Pater's distinguished essays on the history of the Renaissance with their marble prose, lit with the mild rose light of the Victorian ebbtide. But these were essays and to have used them as a model would not have taken me as far as I wanted to go. Then there was, of course, Strachey himself who had purported to present an aspect of the Victorian era through his four portraits, Florence Nightingale, General Gordon, Thomas Arnold and Cardinal Manning, and in doing so had undoubtedly escaped from the lacklustre of mere chronicle and created a work that crackled and sparkled like those faggots lit to consume the protagonist of some old and outdated doctrine. It occurred to me for my book that if I could take a number of characters typical of the era I was writing about and bring them to life on the page, at least I would have something to be going on with while I was establishing the form the book would eventually take.

But my goodness what a task was there! Yeats, Synge, O'Casey, Lady Gregory, James Stephens, James Joyce, Padraic Colum, George Moore, George Russell (AE), Oliver St John Gogarty, Seumas O'Sullivan, Lennox

Robinson for a start; then undoubtedly the young writers of the twenties, Sean O'Faolain, Frank O'Connor, Liam O'Flaherty, Francis Stuart, demanded attention; and the emergence of the poets F.R. Higgins, Patrick Kavanagh and Austin Clarke would have to be dealt with, as well as somewhere or other Mary Lavin, Flann O'Brien, Benedict Kiely, Brendan Behan and James Plunkett. Though I diligently ploughed my way through the works and lives of these different writers it became clear that a work which would encompass them all could not avoid becoming a mere chronicle and that the essential ingredients which had caused the emergence of this last Renaissance in Europe would not be there. Yet I laboured away at the lot of them, putting unfinished portraits away on the shelf, often with a sinking feeling that somehow or other I might not need them in the end.

Then one day a friend remarked to me what perhaps I should have seen from the start, that a Renaissance is a re-birth – or a flowering – and that once I had dealt with the actual events, those which occurred afterwards would speak for themselves. In other words Kavanagh and O'Casey, O'Faolain, O'Flaherty, O'Connor *et al* were the natural result of the forces which had initiated this great revival.

I set out then to take as my period 1852 to 1904, 1904 being the date of the opening of the Abbey Theatre in which it seemed to me so many of the talents of the men of genius of that time had come together. Even those who rejected the Abbey movement, as Joyce did, in their own way would provide a counterpoint to illuminate the period even further. The reason I started with 1852 was that it was the year of both Lady Gregory's and George Moore's births. The seven figures that I selected Strachey-like as typical of the age were Yeats, Lady Gregory, Synge, George Moore, Edward Martyn, George Russell and James

Joyce. These would be my major characters. But some minor ones had to be sketched in too – and here I worked to bring up Standish O'Grady, Douglas Hyde, John O'Leary, Arthur Symons (Yeats's Charon in the underworld of French symbolism), Horace Plunkett and Maud Gonne – Yeats's beloved. It soon became clear that Wilde and Shaw would have to make an appearance too, even though their milieu was London and not Dublin.

Yes indeed, sixteen characters was quite a lot to call before the mind's eye and to have moving around on the canvas that I hoped to create. But just to take my seven major ones, simply to bring them alive was not enough. What I would tell of them had to be subordinate to the main purpose of the book, which was to convey the exhilaration and energy of the period they lived in. I had abandoned the idea of simply presenting a series of portraits as Strachey did and was determined, having made my characters come alive, to have them also meet one another and intermingle as they would in a novel.[1] But I set myself one rule. To bind myself to the wheel of fact. I had taken Desmond MacCarthy's admirable injunction to heart: 'A biographer is an artist who is on oath.'[2]

I determined to use no conversation or event that had not been recorded in books of reminiscences or else that I had heard myself from the lips of those who had lived in the period. This was my masterplan. To execute it was another day's work. At times I was in despair. That half way through the book (with four years' work behind me) I was doubtful of completing it I can confirm from a journal kept between autumn 1980 and February 1981 when I was living in Alicante trying to get a 'scaffolding' for the book into place.

11 December 1980 (Alicante):
Walked 1 1/4 miles on sea front.

Lovely sun but full of doubts.
I have to find a form at which to aim.
Malta, Tangier. I have four years behind me now. I should know what *not* to do. But the size, where is the key.
DREAD. I can't abandon it. I can only grasp the size of the undertaking as I watch it unfold.
I don't have the prescience of architectural foresight. Am I harnessed for five years more. God.

12 December 1980:
It is impossible to record the confusion and despair of writing a biography. Nothing seems possible. The whole world has to be turned upside down – towards one purpose.

At one stage I almost succumbed to the temptation of resorting to faction, that seductive literary device which I referred to in Chapter 1 where invented dialogue and situations are attached to central characters. I actually went out and bought a number of books which specialize in this genre. Fortunately a few sentences from Irving Stone's *The Agony and the Ecstasy*, a 'biographical novel' of Michelangelo, quickly dissuaded me from inventing conversations and situations for my characters.

'What fell on your nose, Michelangelo?'
'A ham.'
'From a butcher's rack? Did you forget to duck?'
'The way the people on Vesuvius forgot to run from the lava: it had covered them before they knew it was coming.'
'Have you ever been in love?'
'. . . in a way.'
'It's always "in a way".'. . .[3]
Her body stirred in its gown, causing a sibilance of the silk. Her fashionably shod foot rested lightly against his calf. His insides somersaulted.[4]

Imagine Yeats having conversations like this with Maud Gonne, or Lady Gregory wooing her lover Wilfrid Blunt with similar gush. No – the temptation wasn't too hard to resist. Perhaps I was rewarded by some guardian angel for resisting this lure (indeed a *roman de scandale* about the period, rich with invented exploits, sexual and otherwise, would likely have had a popular success) for after many weeks and months of apparently hopeless effort gradually it did seem that something was emerging on the canvas.

> **1 February 1981 – Alicante:**
> I hardly dare to write this but last night the machine began to move into motion. I feel I have the storyline. I won't know until I read it over and over again. This is what is so *scaring*. You feel waves of generality beating against the brain waiting to be worked into prose. But this can only happen when the form is there. I don't know how many times I will have to rewrite before getting a readable prose structure. You can only hope then that a form will be born. Let's hope this is the beginning.

Whether it was or not is for others to judge rather than myself. What I am trying to say is that the approach I used was deliberate – what Virginia Woolf called the rainbow-like intangibility of the imaginative approach as opposed to the solid granite one of the chronicler.

I have discussed in the previous chapters the decisions that a biographer has to arrive at in including matters about the private life of his subject, and have argued that if they are necessary to the shaping of the portrait they should be included provided they are kept in perspective. A question however which must always concern the biographer is to what extent he has to take into account the matter of living relatives and their susceptibilities. It seems fair to say that this decision can have something to do with the sort of person who is the subject of the biography. The great statesman, writer or artist has after all placed himself in the public domain to an extent that, in order fully to comprehend his position in relation to the circumstances and age that bred and shaped him, it may well be necessary to deal with material that many relatives and friends would prefer to see left alone.

I had to arrive at certain decisions in relation to this problem of living relatives in two biographies I wrote, and in one of them I think I came to a correct conclusion and in the other the wrong one. When I commenced my biography of Brendan Behan,[5] the poet and playwright, in 1966, I included material which I believe I was justified in using, while in my earlier biography of Oliver St John Gogarty,[6] the poet and wit, I excluded an episode on the grounds of supposed family susceptibilities, which I now feel I should have used.

In Behan's case it became clear after I had begun to interview a number of his friends and associates, that where matters of sex were concerned, he was attracted to his own as well as to the opposite sex. It was more an excess of appetite than a particular preference for one sex or the other. He was, in fact, sexually attracted to women more than men. But long periods of his life had been spent in Borstal or in prison, and in the confinement of such male enclaves he had experimented in order to assuage an unusually active sexual drive. By nature an extrovert, he not only made no secret of his sexual athleticism but boasted openly of it. He would, for instance, at church occasions such as weddings and funerals make great play of the attractions of the choir boys who had sung throughout the service and afterwards, if reproved for his enthusiasm, he would justify himself with stories of 'porthole duff' in the British Navy, of how the German Army had encouraged it in cadet schools, or how the British public schools had created such an ethos in order to produce leaders. Finally, he would assert that most of the boxers he had known 'were bent anyway'. Indeed, as Ben Kiely has recalled, Brendan, contrary to having any regret about his wide range of sexual indulgence, would assert that it was a necessary activity in prison or after 'forty days at sea': 'Listen, Ben, for Jasus' sake, do you see that young soldier over there, you'd take him before you'd take Eleanor Roosevelt.'[7]

With such evidence available to me (and much more indeed) it seemed to me that if I suppressed references to Brendan's bisexual tendencies I would not be creating a true portrait of a character that would, so to speak, take root in my reader's mind and achieve my purpose of transmitting his personality on the page. On the other hand, I had to be aware that a disclosure of this kind about one who had such fame in the public eye could cause comment of a sort that might easily be sensationalized by the popular press. In the end I devoted but a page and a half to this aspect of Behan's life and treated with what I thought was a certain discretion the considerable mass of information that I had come by on the matter.

Alas, what I feared happened. An (to my mind) indiscreet letter to the press before publication, which was not of my making, set reporters on the track so that headlines such as 'The Quare Fella was Queer' and 'Behan was Bent' made the matter a top news item in the British press for a week or so. I was staying at the time in the Savoy Hotel at the expense of the newspaper which had undertaken to serialize the book. So great was the interest aroused by the publication of the initial letter that I had to leave the hotel and return to Ireland in order to avoid reporters from other papers who clamoured for interviews which I was not permitted to give (even had I wanted to) because of my commitment to the newspaper which had bought the serial rights to the book. On my way to the airport some instinct made me think of Brendan's brother, Dominic, who was at that time living in Crawley, a suburb of London, and who must have been wondering about the *brouhaha* about his brother in the paper. I had no copy of the book in my possession at the time but, by a happy chance, Messrs W.H. Smith's bookshop at the airport had, with their usual perspicacity, reacted to the controversy in the newspapers by securing advance copies of the book for sale there. I obtained one of these copies on arriving at Heathrow and despatched it by taxi to Dominic. It was fortunate that I had done so because he had already been contacted by Atticus in the *Sunday Times* and, having been given, no doubt, a somewhat stark version of what appeared in the book, had intimated that he would 'break my jaw again', a reference to the fact that I had only recently recovered from an injury received in a mêlée in Dublin. However, having received the book from me and read it, Dominic was good enough to contact Atticus and tell him that he thought the book was a fair and agreeable account of his brother's character and life. Thwarted by Dominic's honest comment, reporters now sought out Brendan's mother, the eighty-one-year-old Kathleen, hoping to obtain some advance comment which would refute in suitable terms the matters discussed in the book. 'Aren't we all human' was the response of this splendid woman who remained a loyal friend to me during the whole controversy and, indeed, until her death in 1985. In fact, the least disturbed by the matter seemed to be the Behan family. At a publisher's party in London, attended by Rory (Brendan's half-brother) and Seamus, the latter came up to me with hand outstretched and with a beaming smile and said 'Congratulations on a great book. Warts and all, as Cromwell said to Sir Peter Lely.' Perhaps the most delicate defence was made in a letter sent to the *Irish Times* (who did not print it) by a good friend of Brendan's, Desmond MacNamara, the sculptor.

Many people must remember Brendan's anecdotes about what he used to describe as his 'Mahaffyism'.[8] Some of them may have been outrageous lies, though they made good telling. Some were more poignant. When he sang about

> the brooks too wide for leaping,
> the lightfoot lads are laid,
> And the rose-lipped maids are sleeping
> In fields where the roses fade[9]

he was singing from the heart.

'You are a man of somewhat Hellenic diversity,' observed the original Ginger Man[10] to Brendan in Paris, many years ago. 'I must have caught it off an Angelica Kaufmann[11] in Dominic Street when I was scraping it down for an undercoat,' was the reply. It was hardly a factual statement, but it wasn't an evasion.

One matter I had set out to deal with in my biography of Brendan had been the destruction of personality that can take place nowadays when the artistic temperament is exposed to media pressure. Even after his death it seemed clear that whatever chemistry Behan evoked in the public mind was still capable of activating itself to present a distorted image of his real persona through the media.

I found myself in a similar position when I came to write the life of Oliver St John Gogarty, the poet and wit. Here I was faced again with the question of family susceptibility. When I was in the middle of the work the subject died, but his wife, Martha Duane Gogarty, was still alive when the book was published in 1964 by Jonathan Cape. She was an elderly lady of regal appearance who lived in a Dublin hotel where retired gentlewomen were accustomed to live out their declining years. Understandably, in such places, gossip occupies a considerable part of the day and any unnecessary adverse reference to Mrs Gogarty in a newly published work on her husband would be bound to be the subject of comment, perhaps not all of it favourable, among her fellow guests in the hotel.

The material which had caused this dilemma came from *The Green Fool* by Patrick Kavanagh, his first novel, published in 1938. In it he described how, as a young man and an aspiring poet, he had called at Surgeon Gogarty's house in Ely Place and, on the door being opened, he '. . . mistook Gogarty's white-robed maid for his wife – or his mistress. I expected every poet to have a spare wife.'[12] The fact that Mrs Gogarty had been mistaken for a 'spare wife' was not in itself a substantial affront. But it certainly was capable of causing her some distress if it were unnecessarily resurrected in the biography of her husband. I decided to leave it out.

Now, had my only relevant reasons for doing so been the ones I have related above I would not feel today that I had transgressed the duty that a biographer owes to his reader, to give a rounded portrait of his subject. But the matter had not ended with the publication of Kavanagh's *The Green Fool* and his reference to Mrs Gogarty. The poet-surgeon had gone to law over the matter and sued Kavanagh and his publisher, Michael Joseph, in the London High Court. Gogarty was awarded £100 damages by a jury in March 1939, a sum which was paid by Kavanagh's publisher. The real damage though was to the young poet's career as an author. The book was withdrawn from print and it was some time before it again became available to the public. Just when he might have gained a reputation which would have set him on the road to recognition, Kavanagh found himself unable to capitalize on that impetus which can initiate a successful career as an author. Now, there is no doubt that Gogarty knew the extent which a libel action could impede or even annihilate a literary career. Two years previously, he himself had been sued in the Dublin High Court by the

Sinclair brothers, a pair of antique dealers, as the result of a passage in his autobiographical *As I Was Going Down Sackville Street*[13] and a jury had awarded the plaintiff £700 damages and costs against the defendant (in today's money almost the equivalent of £20,000). The book had been withdrawn from circulation and Gogarty had had the bitter experience of finding his brilliant and original work unavailable in the book stores, so that not only was his pocket affected but his literary career as well. Why would he have inflicted a similar punishment on a fellow author for what seemed a trivial matter? There is reason to believe that Gogarty may have become the victim at that time of certain paranoic obsessions about publishers and their origins and believed that by getting at Michael Joseph he was in some way repaying the injury done to himself at an earlier date. But what about the damage done to the young poet? That Gogarty should have shown himself insensitive to this, to say the least of it, is a matter relating to his personality and should have been examined in its proper place in the narrative to complete the portrait I was attempting to present.

Curiously enough, Patrick Kavanagh himself seemed to be the last person to be put out about the matter. He approached me in his casual way in McDaid's bar in 1966 and did something he rarely did to anyone, paid me a compliment on the recent biography. As he was going away he asked me, as if it had just occurred to him, why I hadn't made reference to the libel action taken against *The Green Fool*. I gave him the reasons I have set out above and he nodded approvingly. He obviously had, like myself, had second thoughts because a year or so later he came up to me in the same casual way and said that he had now thought about the matter and felt that I should have referred to the libel action as indeed it had adversely affected his career.

Such are some of the problems that a writer wishing

to approach biography as a work of art may expect to encounter, faced with the resolution of decisions which had he adhered to the device of meticulous chronology he would have been spared. Certainly, some of the writers I have chosen to represent the artist's approach to biography have produced flawed works, but there is about each of their portraits that distinct aura of personality which can only be achieved if the facts are forged in the heat of the imagination. With the present huge output of biography, it will become more and more important to make this distinction. The public has an appetite for supping with the great. Popular biography can make the reader feel that he is partaking in the imaginative process which drives the artist without obliging his reader ever to read a book, attend a play, see a picture or listen to a musical work by the subject of the biography. This makes it all the more important presently to try and evaluate principles which will establish a distinction between two genres which have no inherent relation to one another.

Epilogue

Had Moore a foreknowledge when he wrote *Hail and Farewell* that the novel might have run its course? In the preface I have posed the question whether the imaginative facility can ever capture reality on the page or whether, as Samuel Beckett has asserted in his essay on Proust, what is obtained is at best a second-hand climax. These are valid questions to ask at a time when, with the progress of science, each day reveals some subterfuge by which we may continue to endure the human condition. But taking it that the artistic imagination can escape the atomization of time and catch something on the page that will survive, is it through the presentation of fact that the imagination may give itself full rein, or will invented plot still claim its adherents?

Gosse created his masterpiece with his biographical portrait of his father. Osbert Sitwell will certainly outlive many novelists of his time. Had Virginia Woolf continued the experiment with *Orlando* what might have emerged? What one is trying to suggest is that the contemporary world can throw up, daily, events beside which even the most fantastic plot a novelist might devise could seem banal. Man has walked on the moon, watched by millions on earth – patients have left the operating table with plastic hearts replacing those of human muscle. Only recently over nine hundred people of varying backgrounds, ranging from professional to working class, queued up willingly to take poison which would kill them from an egomaniac evangelist in Guyana.

One cannot imagine that either Rousseau or Baudelaire would have difficulty in assimilating the fantastic nature of contemporary events into the imaginative process. They had been the first to liberate personality from social and religious convention and to commence the voyage into self, without regard for what perils it might entail. In direct line from them, Byron, Gautier, Dostoevsky, Ibsen, Rimbaud and Camus took up the task of exploring the human condition unfettered by categorized convention or traditional belief. Rimbaud, following in the footsteps of Baudelaire whom he termed his 'king of poets, a true God', went so far as to martyr himself on the cross of experience, a sort of saint of vice to further the adventure in consciousness ('Il s'agit d'arriver à l'inconnu par la dérèglement de *tous les sens*').[1]

Stéphane Mallarmé, perhaps with the innate caution of his profession (he was a schoolteacher), held a similar creed but would only allow glimpses of it through the veil of his verse. But when his *L'Après-midi d'un faune*[2] reached the stage in Nijinsky's scenario and choreography,[3] the infuriated public recognized for the first time its true meaning and its relation to the philosophy implicit in Baudelaire's 'Femmes Damnées'[4] and the threat, inherent in the fantastic dancer's crackling movements on the apron stage; and as is often the fashion in Paris, they rose from their seats and proceeded to demolish the auditorium.

But by the time Camus' Mersault arrived in fiction, he had already become a character of his time; young people in Europe and the United States would have

105

little difficulty in identifying their predicament with that of the leading character in *The Outsider*.[5] Mersault was 'cool' – indifferent to his mother's death, race, religion, even to his own fate.

Nietzsche had found it impossible to conceive of a saint in the religious sense.[6] Camus had no such difficulty in finding a contemporary counterpart to the Christian saint. He has given us Dr Bernard Rieux in *La Peste* (*The Plague*) who risks his life to save the plague-ridden population, simply because 'it's a matter of common decency'.[7] Darwin had removed one crutch, Freud another. Much occurred in between. As a result, social awareness has matured to such an extent that the gap between the writer of fiction and his reader has narrowed.

Frederick Karl has written:

> What Baudelaire indicated about the Dandy, Freud suggested about himself, in that both created a cult of 'oneself', a unique individual whose unconscious, once penetrated, revealed an unduplicatable work.[8]

May it not be that the creation of that 'self' in literary form will more likely happen in the future through factual narrative and life writing than through the fictional process? If this is so, biography will form an important part of the writer's output and he will upgrade the value of fact and altering perhaps but slightly its perspective lend it the character of a work of art.

I have described here how biography has reached out to embody within itself something of the nature of art – and I have provided, I hope, some glimpses of how contemporary works of fiction have taken on board aspects of the biographical approach. It seems likely that somewhere or other a fusion between the two will be accomplished. Then we will talk as ever of a 'new art form' and there will be pages for the critics to fill and volumes for the thesis writers to wallow in contentedly and everybody will be happy – till the next time.

Appendix 1

The Good and the Beautiful

The distinction between the good and the beautiful which I have used to structure the central argument in this book, in so far as it has been taken from one discipline and applied to another, may not be as easy to keep before the mind's eye as it should be.

It may be useful therefore to have a look at how two writers of pseudo-philosophical bent, James Joyce and Gerard Manley Hopkins, made out when they took on board scholastic notions in an attempt to create an aesthetic which would justify their literary beliefs, and what conclusions they had arrived at, concerning truth and beauty.

Poets venturing into the aesthetic breach have frequently emerged with pikes bent in the fray. However, an unsound theory of art does not necessarily preclude good literature, so powerful is the imaginative faculty in clearing detritus from its way as it moves towards the creation of a work of art. What is striking, however, about the thinking of Joyce and Hopkins, is that both of them adapted an already existing aesthetic to justify their view that there is no distinction between *bonum* and *pulchrum*, and that the aesthetic experience can result from the simple perception of form alone. In Joyce's case he actually went so far as to attempt to use Aquinas's own writings to establish a premise quite different from that which the philosopher himself had laid out.

Hopkins does not appear to have adverted to any writings of Duns Scotus on the theory of the beautiful (Scotus in any event barely touched on the subject) but simply adapted Scotus' theory of the relationship between matter and form (which differed from Aquinas's hylomorphic theory) to justify his discovery of what he terms 'inscape'.

There is more excuse for Joyce than Hopkins, as the former was an amateur as far as philosophy went, picking his way through phrases from the massive *Summa Theologica* through which the theory of the beautiful is scattered only as an element of a colossal structure. Hopkins on the other hand, during the fourteen tortuous years of training required for his ordination as a Jesuit priest, would have had a thorough academic grounding in philosophy, and his discovery of Duns Scotus would have been preceded by a rigorous training in this discipline.

First Joyce and Aquinas. Joyce devotes four pages of *A Portrait of the Artist as a Young Man* to dealing with his interpretation of Aquinas's theory of beauty (207, 209, 211, 213). On page 211 he has Stephen Dedalus say to his goliard-like and rabelaisian friend Lynch as they walk across the city:

> To finish what I was saying about beauty ... the most satisfying relations of the sensible must therefore correspond to the necessary phases of artistic apprehension. Find these and you find the qualities of universal beauty. Aquinas says: *Ad pulchritudinem tria requiruntur integritas, consonantia, claritas.* I translate it so: *Three things are needed for beauty: wholeness, harmony, and radiance.* Do these correspond to the phases of apprehension? Are you following?

Of course, I am, said Lynch. If you think I have an excrementitious intelligence run after Donovan and ask him to listen to you.

Stephen pointed to a basket which a butcher's boy had slung inverted on his head.

Look at that basket, he said . . .

In order to see that basket, said Stephen, your mind first of all separates the basket from the rest of the visible universe which is not the basket. The first phase of apprehension is a bounding line drawn about the object to be apprehended. An aesthetic image is presented to us either in space or in time. What is audible is presented in time, what is visible is presented in space. But, temporal or spatial, the aesthetic image is first luminously apprehended as selfbounded and selfcontained upon the immeasurable background of space or time which is not it. You apprehended it as *one* thing. You see it as one whole. You apprehend its wholeness. That is *integritas*.[1]

Now in Chapter 1 (p.12) I have dealt with the distinction Aquinas makes between the good and the beautiful, between *bonum* and *pulchrum*.

For Aquinas the act of cognition involves satisfaction when the perception of form through matter is achieved by the mind. This is *bonum* or the good. '*Bonum est quod omnia appetunt*' . . . It is the mind's function to abstract form from matter and when this occurs the mind is satisfied. But when, in the process of abstraction, the mind is spared the least difficulty by the harmonious relations of the parts to one another, as occurs in the perception of the beautiful, then, in addition to being satisfied, the mind is also pleased. It has had an easy ride, so to speak. '*Pulchra enim dicuntur quae visa placent*' ('We call beautiful those things which give pleasure when they are seen).

If we accept then this distinction, it will become clear that Joyce's 'basket' could not be included in Aquinas's definition of the beautiful but would pertain rather to his definition of the good. For Joyce the apprehension of form alone, the perception of the object's separation 'from the rest of the visible universe' – its 'whatness' – will arouse an aesthetic response: whereas Aquinas clearly required another dimension before he would allow the attribution of the beautiful. One might in scholastic terms say that the apprehension of 'the basket' would arouse content or satisfaction, but not the 'pure Joy' which Mercier says results from the contemplation of the beautiful. (D. Mercier, 'Du beau dans la nature et dans l'art', *Revue néo-scholastique*, 2, 1895, p.339)

Another way of stating the proposition would be that the beautiful can only be known through the process of apprehending the good, but the apprehension of the good in itself does not necessarily arouse the sensation brought by the perception of the beautiful. Had Joyce had more than a superficial acquaintance with scholastic thought he therefore would have recognized that the response he was attempting to define related rather to Aquinas's definition of the good than to the beautiful.

Though the 'aesthetic' parts of *A Portrait of the Artist as a Young Man* and *Stephen Hero* are liberally sprinkled with quotes from Aquinas, it would have been impossible for Joyce to read the whole of the *Summa Theologica* or even the section dealing with Aquinas's hylomorphic theory on which his aesthetic is based. As I mentioned earlier, Aquinas's aesthetic theory is not collected under a single heading. He did not, for instance, include the beautiful among the transcendentals, nor did he deal with it in detail as he does with *unum, bonum* and *verum*. It is known that as well as attending occasional philosophy lectures at University College, Joyce used a Latin tag book in the National Library for his ferreting out of Aquinas's aesthetic maxims (and later did some browsing at the Bibliothèque Sainte-Geneviève) and it is probably by using this approach without grasping the full import of the system on which they were based that he succeeded in confusing himself and generations of readers of his work with his notions of the scholastic concept of the beautiful.[2]

Gerard Manley Hopkins would not have had any great acquaintance with Aquinas after he joined the Jesuit Order in 1868 since the Jesuit philosopher Suarez and not Aquinas, a Dominican, was still required reading for Jesuit novices. But Hopkins was on the lookout for some structure on which to hang his instinctively perceived theories of the beautiful. At an early stage in his writing career, indeed before he became a Jesuit, Hopkins had worked out a basic philosophical structure to encompass his theory of the beautiful. In 1868, during a tour of Switzerland, he observed a pattern among the hill clouds and mountains for which he used the word 'inscape' which meant for him the perception of the interior form, a reflection of the divine plan. The effect of 'inscape' he termed 'instress' which seems to have been an attempt to define, as well as the aesthetic response, an accession of divine grace. Writing about Parmenides in his notebooks in 1868 he is impressed by that philosopher's '. . . feeling for instress, for the flush and foredrawn, and for inscape . . .'[3]

In his notebooks, page 143, we find Hopkins writing:

> But such a lovely damasking in the sky to-day I never felt before. The blue was charged with simple instress.[4]

It was after he had begun his novitiate as a Jesuit that Hopkins discovered the Opus Oxoniense of Duns Scotus, from which he took a notion of matter and form which seemed to suit admirably his own theory of inscape.

> At this time I had first begun to get hold of the copy of Scotus on the Sentences in the Baddely Library and was flush with a new stroke of enthusiasm. It may come

to nothing or it may be a mercy from God. But just then when I took in any inscape of the sky or sea I thought of Scotus.[5]

These notions occur often in Hopkins' poems.

I kiss my hand
To the stars, lovely-asunder
Starlight, wafting him out of it; and
Glow, glory in thunder;
Kiss my hand to the dappled-with-damson west:
Since, tho' he is under the world's splendour
and wonder,
His mystery must be instressed, stressed;
For I greet him the days I meet him, and bless when
I understand.

Stanza 5, *The Wreck of the Deutschland* (1875)

It was perhaps shortly after Hopkins' reading of Scotus that an amazed gardener at Stonyhurst, where Hopkins was a novice, observed him walking round and round a stone, scrutinizing it from all angles; presumably he was waiting for the propitious moment when its form would shine forth and be revealed to him.[6]

It is clear that Hopkins felt that Scotus' notion that matter and form are distinct formal principles within the same substance and that there is an instinctive perception of the individual as distinct from the universal, had provided him with a justification for his theory of 'inscape'.[7]

But in pointing out that in Scotus' era (1264–1308) there was 'no scholastic aesthetic', Professor Tatarkiewiez (*History of Aesthetics*, Vol. II, The Hague, Paris, Warsaw, 1970) has shown the limitation imposed by Scotus' theory of individual form as a basis for the development of a theory of beauty.

... as Scotus stated it, besides its generic form, everything has an individual form (haecceitas). It might

112

seem that intuitionism and individualism offered a more favourable basis for aesthetics than the intellectualism of the earlier scholastics; but if all cognition is intuitive and individual, there is no longer anything distinctive about aesthetic cognition.

Aquinas, on the other hand, believed that form 'cannot exist without matter' (*Sine materia existere non potest*), Gent. 1.51. The notion of this unity of matter and form is well set out by D. Nys, in Mercier's *Modern Scholastic Philosophy*.[8]

Poets are seldom at their best in foraging among philosophic systems for ideas to buttress their art. What is interesting is that both Joyce and Hopkins were determined to find justification for their own intuitive reaction to the external world in the works of two philosophers. In concluding that the perception of form alone is sufficient to arouse an aesthetic response, Joyce succeeded in misrepresenting Aquinas, while Hopkins read into Scotus' notion of form an interpretation which had not been developed by the philosopher himself as a theory of beauty.

It is nevertheless important to remember that when Aquinas made his distinction between the good and the beautiful he was not belittling the good. He was simply asserting that when form arranged in a harmonious way shines forth from matter, it does so with a degree of intensity that is not present when the mind in the act of cognition simply discerns the good.

Appendix 2

Getting at the Facts

In the chapter 'Personal Record', I have remarked how the chemistry that Brendan Behan evoked in the public mind was still capable, even after his death, of presenting a distorted image of his real persona. One of the major difficulties in arriving at a satisfactory assessment of Behan's character was that in his autobiographical memoirs he had written and dictated descriptions of his own activities that on subsequent investigation turned out to be inaccurate and at times even downright untrue.

One particular episode in his life and the facts surrounding it serve to illustrate the difficulty facing a biographer who is attempting to obtain an insight into the personality of his subject and is in hot pursuit of material to help him in his task.

On 10 April 1942, Brendan Behan was charged before the Special Criminal Court in Dublin with the attempted murder of a policeman and, having being found guilty, received a sentence of fourteen years' penal servitude. I interviewed seven different people who were present at the actual shooting and, as well, made a routine detailed research of legal documents and the newspaper accounts connected with the case. If we look at Behan's version, and compare it with that of other witnesses, it can provide a useful insight into the difficulties facing a biographer who is attempting to discover what actually happened in a particular situation which may be crucial to the authenticity of the portrait he is trying to create.

As Brendan described in *Confessions of an Irish Rebel*, he had attended an IRA commemoration at Glasnevin Cemetery on Easter Sunday 1942. After the event he was with a friend, Dick Flaherty, when he saw a number of Special Branch policemen approach three IRA men, Andrew Nathan, Lazarian Mangan and Joseph Buckley. According to Behan's account, Special Branch detectives in plain clothes went to arrest Andrew Nathan. Behan threw off his overcoat and went to attack the police with his fists. He then heard someone shout: 'That man has a gun.' When he looked around he saw an IRA man with a revolver who was in a hysterical state and who was screaming, 'I'll use it, I'll use it.' According to Brendan he then snatched the revolver from the IRA man's hand to stop him using it, after which the police opened fire. Brendan fired back at the police to protect himself and subsequently made his escape.

The full extract from Brendan's account in *Confessions of an Irish Rebel* (Hutchinson, 1965), pages 31 and 32, runs as follows:

> The hungry-faced police jumped out of their cars and went to arrest Andrew, Lasarian and Joseph. They gathered around them and looked as if they were going to go mad any minute. My stomach was trying to get rid of my dinner and a cold sweat broke out on me. All at once I threw off my overcoat and went to attack them with my fists. 'Come on, we'll fix this bloody shower,' I said to Cafferty. Everyone was shouting and saying things and one big ugly-faced policeman going mad

with the temper, and shouting himself to tell them to shut up, when all of a sudden somebody screamed, 'That man has a gun,' and I looked round and saw the steel glint of a revolver in one of the I.R.A. officers' hand and he was altogether hysterical. 'I'll use it, I'll use it,' he screamed. Christ, said I in my own mind, why wasn't I back in Borstal, or Feltham Boys' Prison, in solitary? At least I would be there in peace and on my own instead of here with my guts twisted up inside me. As I snatched the revolver out of the officer's hand, the police opened fire. I didn't, and not until they opened fire did I fire back at them and, still firing, Cafferty and I made a desperate run for it.

As there were a number of people who were well placed to give an account of what happened as they saw it, if I could interview them I could then set their versions of the event against Behan's own account.

First of all there was Andrew Nathan, the IRA volunteer whom the police arrested and whom they had in custody when the shooting took place.

The actual IRA volunteer, Lazarian Mangan, who produced the gun, I did not meet. But his elder brother Seamus Mangan, also in the IRA, who was present at the cemetery that day, was able to give a very useful account of what Lazarian had told him afterwards. In addition, Seamus Mangan himself, who was Brendan's superior officer in the IRA, had been responsible for his safety while he was on the run from the police from 5 April until 10 April when he was arrested. His account of what happened in those five days proved invaluable. Other IRA men at Glasnevin that day who were interviewed were Dick Flaherty, who escaped after the shooting with Brendan, Martin Quearney and Ultan O'Neill.

I had a number of meetings with Detective Martin Hanrahan, the policeman at whom Behan had fired two shots and who had subsequently fired back at Behan.

I interviewed Detective Jim Donegan who also took part in Behan's subsequent arrest. Detective Doran's deposition for the trial at the Special Criminal Court came into my hands and proved enormously useful. I obtained, in addition to Detective Doran's deposition, a copy of all the other depositions relating to the police evidence at the trial.

It became clear as I correlated these interviews and depositions and researched the appropriate newspaper accounts of the event that there were two quite different versions of what happened that day. One was Behan's as described in *Confessions of an Irish Rebel* and the other version was that compiled from the descriptions of the persons I have mentioned above.

In Behan's version, he made himself out to be the innocent party who tried to stop Lazarian Mangan firing at the police by snatching the revolver from him and who only fired back at the police after they had first fired at him, despite his attempt to pacify Mangan.

The scenario as outlined by the other witnesses I interviewed was quite different. As this ran, it would seem that Mangan had not intended to use the gun or at worst had hesitated and that Behan, infuriated by his pusillanimity, had shouted at Mangan: 'Shoot the fucking bastards.' And when Mangan showed no signs of doing this Behan grabbed the gun from him and fired at Detective Martin Hanrahan, the bullet piercing the sleeve of the policeman's overcoat. Then he and another IRA man, Dick Flaherty, made their escape, and were on the run for five days between 5 April and 10 April.

Not only was Behan's account of the shooting undermined by the evidence which emerged from other sources, but he seems also to have given a totally untrue account of what happened during the period he was at large, as well as concocting a scenario for his arrest which had no basis in fact. His descriptions, between pages 32 and 46, of his adventures while evading the police seem to have been largely imaginary. Finally, his account of his arrest as given in his book, with himself in his bed Jesse James fashion, confronted by the marshals and unable to reach for his gun, is completely at variance with what those who actually arrested him were able to tell me.

Thus there were four separate sections of the episode which had to be examined: (1) the shooting incident at Glasnevin; (2) the events which took place that evening involving Behan and the IRA's efforts to prevent his arrest by the police; (3) the events which took place during the five days he was at large; (4) the manner of his arrest.

First let us take a look at the other accounts of the shooting affair at Glasnevin on 5 April 1942. Here is Andrew Nathan's version. (It will be remembered that Andrew Nathan was the first IRA man arrested by the police and it was his apprehension which led to Mangan producing his gun).

> When we got to De Courcey Square, Joe Buckley, Laz Mangan and myself were there. The special police moved in on me. Laz went out into the road. He pulled out a gun as the police came to him. Brendan took the gun off Laz, threw his coat on the ground and was frothing at the mouth. He said: 'Shoot the bastards, shoot the bastards.' We were just near Croppys Acre. There were two policemen near me holding me and the bullets which were fired at the policemen were not too far away from me. We were tried on April 25th before a Special Criminal Court, the three of us together presided over by Colonel Joyce. Brendan got fourteen years for attempted murder, I got seven years for possession of a weapon and Buckley got five years for being in the IRA. [Interview with author]

When I interviewed Detective Martin Hanrahan his account bore out Nathan's in almost every detail:

On the road outside the cemetery Detectives Doran and Donegan moved in on Nathan. Laz Mangan in the meantime had sprung away in the middle of the road, pulling out his revolver. He stood there unable to make up his mind what to do and Brendan came down the road frothing with excitement. He threw his overcoat and his jacket and waistcoat all off in one throw and he was standing in his shirtsleeves in the middle of the road, shouting: 'Give me the gun and I will shoot the bastards' to Mangan. Then he grabbed the revolver and fired it at me just as I was coming on the scene with Detective Kirwan. One of them pierced my overcoat underneath the arm. Brendan was about ten yards away but he ran off followed by an IRA colleague. I fired after Brendan as he disappeared and then me and Donegan set off after him. I was going to fire again but I saw women and children and Brendan running through them. I had taken first place in the Irish Police championship as a sharpshooter. I suppose I could have plugged Brendan but I didn't want to take the chance of killing him if I took a deliberate shot.

I was not able to get in touch with Detective Garda Richard Wilmot but managed to obtain a copy of his deposition for the court. His account is as follows:

Before he reached Mangan he saw Mangan take a gun from his overcoat pocket and present it as if to fire. Mangan was called on by Detective Garda Kirwan to drop the gun. At this stage Brendan Behan rushed up and said to Mangan, 'Give me that gun and I will shoot the bastards', at the same time taking the gun from Mangan and divesting himself of overcoat and jacket coat proceeded to fire in the direction of Detective Gardaí Hanrahan and Kirwan. Behan then ran in the direction of De Courcey Square followed by Detective Gardaí Hanrahan, Goodwin and Kirwan.

Seamus Mangan, Lazarian Mangan's brother, who was at the funeral and in the vicinity of De Courcey Square but who did not see the actual events, nevertheless had many conversations with his brother Lazarian about what happened.

> Laz hesitated to shoot [Seamus told me] because, as he told me after he was released from jail, the detective approaching him had no gun in his hand and in his own words 'I could not shoot an unarmed man.' However the issue was decided before he could make up his mind by Brendan seizing the gun from his hand and releasing two shots. This hesitation to shoot an apparently unarmed man was quite in consonance with the ideals of chivalry inculcated into these young men in the Fianna apart from the fact that there was a general HQ order forbidding armed resistance to arrest.

That the police there themselves believed that Mangan had no intention of using his gun is evident from the fact that he was charged only with possession and received a seven-year sentence, while Brendan Behan was charged with attempted murder and sentenced to fourteen years' penal servitude.

Now we come to the events immediately following the shooting and Behan's escape with Dick Flaherty. As described in *Confessions of an Irish Rebel*, after the shooting they jumped over a wall and ran for it. After various adventures they settled down for the night 'in a terrible slum place' where a lady gave them rugs and cushions to sleep on the floor. They then had to 'leave their native city and make for the border before the sun had the heart to get up that Sunday morning'. Brendan gives a detailed account of his stay in Belfast which according to him extended over a month and during which he attended weddings and parties, and in between did 'a few little shootings here and there'.

According to his account he and Flaherty remained in Belfast until the 'heat blew off' and then returned to Dublin some months later where they raided pawn shops and lodged in the house of an ex-British soldier.

As Behan was only five days at large before his capture his own account which takes in an extended period is clearly inaccurate. That it is in fact false is attested to by Seamus Mangan who was Behan's superior officer having the responsibility of helping him to avoid arrest – it was possible that if Behan were brought to trial he could have been executed under the law as it stood at that time.

Here is Seamus Mangan's account (as related to the author):

When I heard of the encounter shortly after it took place that afternoon it was rumoured that someone was wounded. This was a serious situation as it meant trial before the Special Military Court and a possible death sentence. I therefore set about two things – trying to organise a rescue, which was very unlikely to get off the ground, and a search party to bring in Brendan. I went to Quearney's to ask them to contact volunteers and then to Mrs Parnell's in North Great George's Street as this was a sort of information centre for republican activities.

After about three hours Brendan arrived into Parnell's which was a large tenement room, with curtained beds and very neat and tidy. He was in his shirt with the gun stuck in the waistband of his trousers. Mrs Parnell gave him her dinner and provided him with a coat. She was a Longford woman (I think), widowed, with one son, Jacky, in jail for the Magazine Fort raid, and another, Freddie, either on the run or in jail.

I then took Brendan to the Castle Hotel in Gardner's Row owned by Donal O'Connor (a Cork or Kerry Republican) to enlist the help of Mick Kelly, a former member of GHQ who had been sentenced to five years for treason felony in the Crown Entry affair in Belfast in 1936. Mick gave Brendan some money and told me to take him to Donlon's house in Hollybank Road in Glasnevin. We also decided to get Brendan over the border to Belfast as he would be safer there, even if arrested, than facing a Free State Court Martial. Mick arranged for me to meet Sean McCool who had been arrested with him in the Crown Entry and was now Chief of Staff. The meeting which was to have been at 4 p.m. in Gardner Street Church, a favourite rendezvous of Sean's, never took place as Sean had already been picked up.

Mick and Brendan and I returned to Parnell's to wait till dark as there was a huge hue and cry and I was told soldiers on the streets. On the way back to Parnell's we passed unexpectedly what we took to be a squad car outside the Belvedere Hotel at the corner of Gardner's Row and North Great George's Street. The driver was in the car and the rest presumably inside searching. We continued on and went into the first tenement with the door open – closing the door behind us. We thought to get out the back but the window was closed by rusty iron bars, which Mick and I tried to break, while Brendan was placed behind a pillar with the gun containing only two rounds. After a time we ventured out and I took Brendan via devious routes and along Phibsboro Road to Donlon's. Donlon was a close relative [or brother-in-law?] of Jim Killeen arrested along with Mick Kelly at Crown Entry Belfast. Donlon's house, also his grocer's shop in Moore Street, were safe retreats which were never discovered and which I subsequently used for Jackie Griffith who was shot in Mount Street. The next day I took away Brendan's gun (a Colt or a Smith and Wesson) which I had been told had been taken from the Magazine Fort and gave him a Smith and Wesson with 18 rounds of ammunition. Brendan was given strict instructions not to leave his safe hideout. However he took to visiting his grandmother and God knows who else. In the meantime we had found out that no one had been wounded in the affray. We also heard that his father, who was a member of the 26th Batt. Volunteers (Free State), had been making a deal for Brendan to give himself up.

About four days afterwards Brendan was seen by a guard at Parnell Street. He drew the gun but no shots were fired and he escaped up Hill Street. He told me this the next day. When I came to my room in a cul de sac down by the river at Island Bridge I found Brendan waiting on the doorstep. I was angry. I asked him how long he'd been there and he said a couple of hours, but he had kept out of sight in a pub on the corner. I took him back to Donlon's where I was told he had dropped the gun in front of the woman of the house who was pregnant and that the gun was now down in the shed or garage. As it was no use there I took it from him. I believe later that night he took off to his Grannie's again and was arrested in Blessington Street. This was April 10th although I did not know this till later. Therefore he was only five days on his keeping or in mine and was never near Belfast.

The IRA man who was on the run with Behan during the five days he was at large was Dick Flaherty. When I interviewed him, while he corroborated that some of the incidents as related by Brendan in *Confessions of an Irish Rebel* (where Flaherty appears under the name of Cafferty) did take place, he denied that they went to Belfast and was quite definite that they never, as Behan said, robbed pawnbrokers' offices of sums such as £2000 and £3000. 'I would never rob a pawn shop,' Flaherty told me, 'those goods belong to the poor.' He said this with some indignation and added: 'Anyway we couldn't 've done it. The pawn shops were on strike in April 1942.' This was confirmed for me by Jim Cummins of Brereton's pawnbrokers in Capel Street, who served his time there in the 1940s.

> There was a strike between September 1941 and October 1942. It was a strike by employees over wages. The shops were picketed by the employees and in the circumstances it would have been impossible for Behan to have robbed a pawn shop. In any event there were no robberies of pawn shops during that period.

He added humorously: 'Anyway I can't see Brendan Behan passing a picket.'

Lastly, there is Brendan's account in *Confessions of an Irish Rebel* of his arrest by detectives after the shooting episode at Glasnevin.

Outside the sun was just beginning on a feeble attempt to come out on this summer's day, 1942 ... I was at Jack Corr's residence in number 15, Blessington Street, Dublin, near to where my great-grandmother and my grandfather lived. I had decided that a bit of light and air would be more to my taste and light and air I got for the asking without moving a muscle.

The door flew open as if the devil himself was behind it, and a lot of mean-faced bastards grabbed me as I made for the window. I was treated to a piece of verbal abuse by Gantley and his minions, but I was not physically assaulted as I had been in Liverpool when I was last arrested. One of the detective officers slipped me a packet of cigarettes and a box of matches, some would say for to soften me up to give information, but I am always prepared to look upon these things as manifestations of human charity. They searched me, putting their hands along the seams of my trousers where they found the gun.

'You wouldn't have come in here so shaggin' easy,' I said, 'if I had had the time to use it. You'll never drive the Irish out of Ireland, and that's for fughing sure.'

Gantley looked at me and sighed, as if he had heard nothing, and with a younger, dark-haired one put the handcuffs on me.

I was taken out to a waiting car where a crowd had now gathered and one of them made a half-hearted attempt to speak to me.

'Come on,' said the dark-haired one, 'move off out of that. There's nothing to see here ...'

We drove to station headquarters where the sergeant wrote down my name and my particulars, and I was put in one of the cells looking out towards the flats, to await trial in the morning.

This account is largely a figment of Brendan Behan's imagination. First of all, it was five days after he had escaped in the middle of April when he was arrested, not some months later and in the summer as he implies here. Secondly, it is clear that he had no gun in his possession at the time as Seamus Mangan had taken the gun from Behan earlier that day.

Detective Officer Donegan who took part in Behan's arrest told me that he had arranged to meet Detective Officer Doran in Blessington Street on the 10th. When he arrived he found that Doran had already encountered Behan in the street and simply arrested him there and then. He had found no gun on Behan. Then they both took him to the station.

Detective Officer Doran's deposition for the Special Court reads:

> At 8.25 pm on the 10th April 1942 I observed Brendan Behan walking along Blessington Street towards North Circular Road. I approached him and I caught hold of his arms and searched him. I asked Behan 'Where is the gun you had,' and Behan replied, 'My colt revolver was taken from me yesterday.'

It would seem then that on four key matters relating to the shooting episode at Glasnevin, Brendan Behan had written a fictitious version of his own involvement in what purports to be an autobiographical memoir based on fact. But it took seven interviews and research into relevant documents to arrive at some coherent account of what actually happened at Glasnevin Cemetery on 5 April 1942 and the subsequent events which took place between that date and 10 April the same year.

It might appear to a reader that in this section of the appendices I have succumbed to the very temptation to overuse the process of information collecting that I have earlier questioned. But even in the collection of information the biographer is not dispensed from exercising the selective faculty. The modern biographer has to train himself to recognize whether a person is telling the truth or not, in much the same way as a barrister has to develop a sense of judgement in accepting the evidence presented to him by his client before deciding how to make use of it in court. Then, of course, the various pieces of information have to be collated and a conclusion arrived at. Often this may amount to little more than a paragraph in a whole book. But that paragraph may play an important, perhaps vital part in the creation of the overall mosaic, and the labour involved in its construction will have been well worth the trouble if a true portrait has been achieved.

Notes

PREFACE

1. Samuel Beckett, *Proust* (New York: Grove Press, 1931); reprint date unknown; p. 49

CHAPTER 1: SELECTOR OR COLLECTOR

1. G. G. Coulton, *Medieval Panorama* (1938), p. 439, as quoted in James Clifford, ed., *Biography as an Art: Selected Criticism 1560–1960* (New York: OUP, 1962)
2. John Aubrey, *Aubrey's Brief Lives* (London: Penguin, [1949] 1982), pp. 282–3
3. Ibid., p.283
4. André Maurois, *Aspects of Biography* (Cambridge: CUP, 1929), p.15
5. John Morley, *The Life of William Ewart Gladstone*, Volume III (London: Macmillan, [1903] 1904), pp. 466–7
6. Ibid., p.485
7. Ibid., p.482
8. Thomas Moore, *The Life of Byron* (1830)
9. Beckett, *Proust*, p.42
10. Lytton Strachey, *Eminent Victorians* (New York: The Modern Library, Random House, 1918), p.vii
11. Lytton Strachey, *Elizabeth and Essex* (London: Chatto and Windus, 1928)
12. Lytton Strachey, *Queen Victoria* (London: Chatto and Windus, 1921)
13. Strachey, *Elizabeth and Essex*, p.16.
14. André Maurois, *Memoirs* (London: The Bodley Head, 1970)
15. Maurois, ibid., p.368

16. André Maurois, *The Quest for Proust*, trans. Gerard Hopkins (London: Penguin, [1949] 1962), p.127
17. Maurois, *Aspects of Biography*, p.62
18. Clifford, ed., *Biography as an Art*, p.ix
19. Thomas Aquinas, *Summa Theologica*. The quotations are taken from: I, q. 5 a 4 ad 1. In the *Summa Theologica*, I–II q.27 a 1 ad 3, Aquinas makes this distinction between the Good and the Beautiful: 'Sed ratione differunt. Nam bonum proprie respicit appetitum; est enim bonum quod omnia appetunt. Et ideo habet rationem finis; nam appetitus est quasi quidam motus ad rem. Pulchrum autem respicit vim cognoscitivam: pulchra enim dicuntur quae visa placent.' (They are different notions none the less. For the good, which is what all desire, properly has to do with appetite. So, too, it has to do with the idea of an end; for appetite is a kind of movement towards an end. Beauty, however, has to do with knowledge, for we call those things beautiful which please us when they are seen.)

Dr Liberato Santoro, of University College, Dublin, has suggested to me that of the three transcendentals, *unum, bonum, verum*, the last is the one most suitable to set in contrast to *pulchrum* for the purpose of the argument I am making here. His feeling is that *verum* 'the exact conformity of the subject perceived, with its mental "type" (*veritas est adequatio rei et intellectus*)' makes the distinction with *pulchrum* ('we call those things beautiful which please us when they are seen') more compelling than that of contrasting it with *bonum* ('the good is what all desire').

He does see a distinction between *bonum* and *pulchrum* in that the first is what he terms 'analytical' and the second 'intuitive'. He further emphasizes this by pointing out that the cognitive process proceeds in the case of *bonum* in 'a labouring way till the movement and the being together become one', while there is no such effort in the apprehension of the beautiful. His solution would be to couple the two in a portmanteau word, *bonum-verum*, which would strengthen the argument in a strictly philosophical presentation.

I am reluctant however to ask the reader to take on board anything which might complicate an already somewhat subtle scholastic distinction and have therefore used *bonum* throughout, while hoping that Professor Santoro's acute observation may be kept in mind.

20. Richard Ellmann, *James Joyce* (1959), new and revised ed. (New York: OUP, 1982)
21. *Selected Letters of James Joyce*, ed. Richard Ellmann (London: Faber & Faber, 1975), p.361
22. The Weaver figures are from: Brenda Maddox, *Nora: A Biography of Nora Joyce* (London: Hamish Hamilton, 1988), pp.

295, 296. The paragraph's concluding quotation is from: *Selected Letters of James Joyce*, op. cit., p.361

23. Arthur Power, *Conversations with James Joyce* (London: Millington, 1974), p.74

24. Nino Frank, 'The Shadow that had Lost its Man' in *Portraits of the Artist in Exile*, ed. Willard Potts (Dublin: Wolfhound Press, 1979), pp. 94, 96

25. Virginia Woolf, *New York Herald Tribune*, 30 October 1927

26. Ibid., pp.149–50

27. Hugh Kenner, 'The Impertinence of Being Definitive' in *Times Literary Supplement*, 17 October 1982, p.1384

28. Michael Holroyd, *Lytton Strachey: A Biography* (London: Penguin, [1967–68] 1980)

29. Gerald Brenan, *Personal Record* (London: Hamish Hamilton, 1975)

30. Holroyd, *Lytton Strachey*, op. cit., p. 889

31. Lytton Strachey, *Eminent Victorians* (New York: The Modern Library, Random House, 1918); *Queen Victoria* (London: Chatto and Windus, 1921); *Elizabeth and Essex* (London: Chatto and Windus, 1928)

32. Michael Holroyd, *Augustus John*, Vols I & II (London: Heinemann, 1974, 1975). I have not included here an examination of Mr Holroyd's biography of Bernard Shaw as the third volume of this work had not appeared before *Biographers and the Art of Biography* had gone to press.

33. Norman Mailer, *Marilyn – A Biography* (New York: Grosset and Dunlap, 1973)

34. Norman Mailer, 'The White Negro' in *Advertisements for Myself* (London: Panther Books, [1968] 1985)

35. Norman Mailer, *The Armies of the Night* (New York: New American Library, 1968)

36. Arthur Rimbaud, letter written to Georges Izambard, *Oeuvres complètes* (Paris: Gallimard Pléiade, 1946), p.252

37. Norman Mailer, *The Naked and the Dead* (New York: Rinehart and Co., 1948)

38. Norman Mailer, *Advertisements for Myself* (Panther, 1985, p.266)

39. Hilary Mills, *Mailer: A Biography* (London: New English Library, [1982] 1983), p.397

40. Fred Guiles, *Norma Jean* (London: W.H. Allen, 1969)

41. Maurice Zolotow, *Marilyn Monroe* (New York, 1962)

42. *Mailer: A Biography*, op. cit., p.399

43. Pauline Kael in the *New York Times Book Review*, 22 July 1973

44. Mike Wallace interview on *60 Minutes* broadcast, 13 July 1973
45. *Marilyn*, p.69
46. *Harper's Magazine*, October 1973
47. Norman Mailer, *The Executioner's Song* (London: Hutchinson, 1979)
48. Conversation with the author, 1972
49. J.P. Donleavy, *The Ginger Man* (New York: McDowell and Obolensky, 1956)
50. Norman Mailer, *An American Dream* (London: Grafton Books, [1972] 1987), p.68
51. *Mailer: A Biography*, op. cit., p.425
52. *The Executioner's Song*, op. cit., p.305
53. *Mailer: A Biography*, op. cit., pp.427, 428
54. *The Executioner's Song*, op. cit., p.345
55. Ibid.
56. Ibid., p.985
57. Norman Mailer, *Miami and the Siege of Chicago* (London: Penguin, [1968] 1969)
58. *The Executioner's Song*, op. cit., p.1053
59. Ibid., p.854
60. Ibid., pp.951–3
61. Truman Capote, *In Cold Blood* (London: Abacus, [1966] 1984)
62. Mailer, *The Armies of the Night*.
63. Truman Capote, *Music for Chameleons* (New York: New American Library, [1975] 1980)
64. Truman Capote, *The Muses are Heard* (New York: Random House, 1956)
65. Capote, *Music for Chameleons*, op. cit., p. xiv
66. Kenneth Tynan, *Tynan Right and Left* (New York: Atheneum, 1967)
67. Interview with Truman Capote in the *Paris Review*, 25 January 1965
68. *In Cold Blood*, op. cit., p.8
69. Ibid., p.38
70. Desmond MacCarthy, *Memories* (London: MacGibbon and Kee, 1953), p.32
71. Gerald Clarke, *Capote: A Biography* (London: Hamish Hamilton, 1988), p.359
72. Clarke, ibid., p.352
73. Ibid., p.331
74. *Music for Chameleons*, op. cit, p. xiii
75. Ibid., p.xv

76. *Mailer: A Biography*, op. cit., p.194
77. Lillian Ross, *Picture* (London: Penguin, [1952] 1962); John Hersey, *Hiroshima* (Penguin, 1946); Cornelius Ryan, *The Longest Day* (London: Coronet, 1987)
78. Osbert Sitwell, *Left Hand, Right Hand!*, 1945; *The Scarlet Tree*, 1946; *Great Morning*, 1948; *Laughter in the Next Room*, (1949). All published in London by Macmillan.
79. Sitwell, *Laughter in the Next Room*, p.243
80. Ibid., p.244
81. Ibid., p.283. Sitwell, *The Scarlet Tree*, p.56
82. Sir George Sitwell, *On the Making of Gardens* (London: John Murray, 1909)
83. Sitwell, *Great Morning*, p.292
84. Sitwell, *Laughter in the Next Room*, p.89
85. Sitwell, *Great Morning*, p.281
86. Sitwell, *Laughter in the Next Room*, p.278
87. Ibid., p.252
88. *The Scarlet Tree*, p.79
89. Proust, *Remembrance of Things Past* in 12 vols. (New York: Random House)

CHAPTER 2: TO TELL OR NOT TO TELL

1. Virginia Woolf, 'The New Biography' in *New York Herald Tribune*, 30 October 1927
2. André Maurois, *Aspects of Biography* (CUP, 1929), p.15
3. L.A.G. Strong, *The Minstrel Boy: A Portrait of Tom Moore* (London: Hodder and Stoughton, 1937), p.232
4. Edmund Gosse, *The Life of Algernon Charles Swinburne* (London: Macmillan, 1917)
5. Ann Thwaite, *Edmund Gosse: A Literary Landscape* (London: Secker and Warburg, 1984), p.480
6. Ibid., p.478
7. Rupert Croft-Cooke, *Feasting with Panthers* (London: W.H. Allen, 1967), pp. 21–2
8. Robert Baldick, ed., *Pages from the Goncourt Journal* (OUP, 1962, 1978), pp. 212–14
9. Edmund Gosse, quoted in *The Aesthetic Adventure*, William Gaunt (Cardinal, 1975), p.175
10. *The Life of Algernon Charles Swinburne*, op. cit.
11. Thwaite, *Edmund Gosse: A Literary Landscape*, op. cit., p.194
12. Ezra Pound, *Poetry* (Chicago) quoted in Thwaite, op. cit., p.479

13. 'The New Biography' in *New York Herald Tribune*, 30 October 1927
14. Ibid.
15. George D. Painter, *Marcel Proust* (London: Penguin, [1959] 1983), pp. 582–8
16. Sigmund Freud, *Art and Literature* (London: Penguin, 1985)
17. Ibid., p.471
18. Hugh Kenner, 'The Impertinence of Being Definitive', in *Times Literary Supplement*, 17 December 1982, p.1384
19. Ellmann, *James Joyce*, revised ed. 1982, p.763
20. James Joyce, *Ulysses* (London: Bodley Head, 1936)
21. Kenner, 'The Impertinence of Being Definitive', op. cit., p.1384
22. Richard Ellmann, *Oscar Wilde* (London: Hamish Hamilton, 1987)
23. Terence Cawthorne FRCS, 'The Last Illness of Oscar Wilde' in *Proceedings of the Royal Society of Medicine* (Section on the History of Medicine), Meeting on 5 November 1958, London
24. Ibid., Vol. 52, p.123
25. Arthur Ransome, *Oscar Wilde: A Critical Study* (London: Martin Secker, 1912), p.199
26. Arthur Ransome, *Oscar Wilde* (London: Methuen, 1913), p.217
27. Lytton Strachey, *Eminent Victorians*, op. cit., pp. 239–341
28. Peter Johnson, *Gordon of Khartoum* (Wellingborough: Stephens, 1985)

CHAPTER 3: WHO DARES WINS

1. See above, Chapter 1.
2. *Daily Mail*, October 1928
3. Virginia Woolf, *Orlando* (London: Penguin, [1928] 1967)
4. The Henry W. and Albert A. Berg collection of English and American Literature, New York Public Library. Quoted in Victoria Glendinning, *Vita: The Life of Vita Sackville-West*.
5. Victoria Glendinning, *Vita: The Life of Vita Sackville-West* (London, 1983), p.181
6. Woolf, *Orlando*, op. cit., p.182
7. Ibid., p.158
8. Leonard Woolf, ed., *A Writer's Diary: Being Extracts from the Diary of Virginia Woolf* (London: Hogarth Press, 1953), p.124
9. E.M. Forster, 'Virginia Woolf', The Rede Lecture, Cambridge University Press; quoted in Quentin Bell, *Virginia Woolf*
10. *A Writer's Diary*, op. cit., p.47

11. Quentin Bell, *Virginia Woolf: A Biography*, Volume Two (London: Hogarth Press, 1972), p.172
12. Virginia Woolf, *Roger Fry: A Biography* (London: The Hogarth Press, 1940)
13. Bell, *Virginia Woolf: A Biography*, Volume Two, op. cit., p.214
14. Woolf, in 'The New Biography' in *New York Herald Tribune*, 30 October 1927.
15. Virginia Woolf to Vanessa Bell, Berg Collection.
16. Bell, *Virginia Woolf: A Biography*, Volume Two, op. cit., p.208
17. *Roger Fry: A Biography*, op. cit., p.25
18. Ibid., p.60
19. Ibid., p.66
20. Woolf, *A Writer's Diary*, op. cit., pp. 299, 300, 314, 317
21. Ibid., p.339
22. Edmund Gosse, *The Life of Philip Henry Gosse FRS* (Kegan Paul, 1890)
23. Edmund Gosse, *Father and Son* (London: Penguin, [1907] 1983).
24. Gosse, *The Life of Philip Henry Gosse*, op. cit.
25. Thwaite, *Edmund Gosse: A Literary Landscape*, op.cit., p.320
26. Letter to Frederic Harrison, quoted in ibid., p.432
27. See quotation from Strachey, op. cit., Chapter 1, n. 10.
28. Gosse, *Father and Son*, op. cit., p.43
29. Ibid., p.94
30. Ibid., pp.94–5
31. Ibid., pp.124–5
32. Ibid., pp.204–5
33. Desmond MacCarthy in the *New Statesman*, April 1917

CHAPTER 4: THE BIOGRAPHER'S WAY I

1. Phyllis Grosskurth, 'An Interview with George Painter' in *Salmagundi*, No. 61, Fall 1983, p.31
2. Ibid.
3. George Painter, *Marcel Proust* (Penguin, [1977] 1983), p.449
4. Samuel Beckett, *Proust* (New York: Grove Press, nd.), p.21
5. Grosskurth, op. cit., p.31
6. *Ulysses* (Penguin, 1972), p.43
7. Marcel Proust, *Swann's Way*, Part Two, trans. C.K. Scott Moncrieff (London: Chatto and Windus, [1922] 1970)
8. Marcel Proust, *By Way of Sainte-Beuve*, trans. Sylvia Townsend Warner (London: Chatto and Windus, 1958), pp.17–19
9. Ibid.
10. See *Freeman's Journal*, 16 June 1904, p.2

11. *Ulysses* (Penguin, 1972), p.296
12. *Irish Worker*, 2 December 1911
13. See Ulick O'Connor archive, University Library, University of Delaware, Newark, Delaware
14. Richard Ellmann, ed., *Selected Letters of James Joyce* (London: Faber and Faber, 1975), p.286

CHAPTER 4: THE BIOGRAPHER'S WAY II

1. George Moore, *Confessions of a Young Man* (London: Penguin, [1918] 1939); James Joyce, *A Portrait of the Artist as a Young Man* (London: Penguin, [1916] 1973); George Moore, *Hail and Farewell*, Richard Cave, ed. (Bucks: Colin Smythe Ltd, [1911] 1976)
2. George Moore, *A Mummer's Wife* (1884) (London: Heinemann, 1933)
3. George Moore, *Impressions and Opinions* (London: David Nutt, 1891)
4. Ibid., pp.98–110
5. George Moore, *Vain Fortune* (London: Walter Scott Ltd, 1895)
6. James Joyce, *Dubliners* (London: Grant Richards, 1914)
7. George Moore, *The Untilled Field* (London: Heinemann, [1903] 1931)
8. *Hail and Farewell*, op. cit., p.236.
9. Ibid., pp.49–50
10. Ibid., p.50
11. Ibid., p.51
12. Ibid.
13. Ibid., p.50
14. Ibid., p.76
15. Ibid., p.190
16. Ibid., p.85
17. Ibid., p.51
18. W.B. Yeats, 'The Countess Cathleen' in *Collected Plays* (London: Macmillan, 1934)
19. *Hail and Farewell*, op. cit., pp.108–9
20. Ibid., p.540
21. Ibid., p.564
22. W.B. Yeats, *Autobiographies* (London: Macmillan, 1955) p.402
23. Ibid., p.452
24. Ibid., pp.404–5
25. Edouard Manet, *Le noyé repêche*, oil painting on canvas.
26. Charles Morgan, *Epitaph on George Moore* (London: Macmillan, 1935), p.2

Notes

CHAPTER 5: PERSONAL RECORD

1. Leon Edel had written a fine group study of the Bloomsbury set but I intended to extend if I could the narrative possibilities that were used in that work – *Bloomsbury, A House of Lions* (London: The Hogarth Press, 1979)
2. Desmond MacCarthy, *Memories*, p.32
3. Irving Stone, *The Agony and the Ecstasy* (London: Methuen, [1961] 1987), p.254
4. Ibid.
5. Ulick O'Connor, *Brendan Behan* (London: Hamish Hamilton, 1970)
6. Ulick O'Connor, *Oliver St John Gogarty* (London: Jonathan Cape, 1964)
7. Personal communication from Benedict Kiely.
8. John Pentland Mahaffy, Professor of Ancient Greek, Trinity College, Dublin, 1880–1919. He is generally held to have had considerable influence on Oscar Wilde's development as a conversationalist, while Wilde was his pupil at Trinity in the 1870s. He had written a history of ancient Greece, the first edition of which dealt frankly with male love in Athens – hence Brendan Behan's use of 'Mafaffyism' to imply homosexual leanings,
9. This was a *mélange* of Kingsley and Housman which Kathleen Behan, Brendan's mother, had fused together for singing purposes.
10. Gainor Crist, original of Sebastian Dangerfield, picaresque hero of *The Ginger Man*, J.P. Donleavy's novel on Dublin in the fifties.
11. This reference would require almost a page to explain adequately. Angelica Kaufmann visited Dublin in the eighteenth century and her paintings were still on the walls and ceilings of eighteenth-century houses in the centre of Dublin when Brendan Behan grew up there. These houses had however become tenements by the turn of the century; thus the reference to 'scraping down' . . . an Angelica Kaufmann.
12. Patrick Kavanagh, *The Green Fool* (London: Michael Joseph, 1938)
13. Oliver St John Gogarty, *As I Was Going Down Sackville Street* (Rich and Cowan, 1937)

EPILOGUE

1. Rimbaud, letter written to Georges Izambard, *Oeuvres complètes*.
2. Stéphane Mallarmé, *L'Après-midi d'un faune* (1876), *The Penguin Book of French Verse* (London: Penguin, 1958)

3. *L'Après-midi d'un faune*. Premièred by Les Ballets Russes in the company's Paris season, 29 May 1912
4. Charles Baudelaire, *Les Fleurs du Mal* (1857)
5. Albert Camus, *The Outsider*, trans. Joseph Laredo (London: Penguin, [1942] 1984)
6. Friedrich Nietzsche, *Beyond Good and Evil*, trans. by Walter Kaufmann (New York: Vintage, 1966)
7. Albert Camus, *The Plague* (London: Penguin, [1947] 1985), p.136
8. Frederick Karl, *Modern and Modernism: The Sovereignty of the Artist 1885–1925* (New York: Atheneum, 1985), p.137

APPENDIX 1

1. Joyce, *A Portrait of the Artist* (Penguin 1967), p.211–12
2. From colleagues at University College such as Felix Hackett, W.G. Fallon and Eugene Sheehy one learnt that Joyce rather prided himself in his first year as an exponent of Aquinas: 'Those souls that hate the strength that mine has/Steeled in the school of old Aquinas.'
It was fashionable to attend philosophy classes at the College whether or not one was reading for a degree in the subject and Joyce certainly seems to have been familiar with two books in the course, Boedder's *Natural Theology* and Rickaby's *General Metaphysics*. Rickaby in fact notes in *General Metaphysics* (p.150, n.45) that 'there are some [De Quincey and Ruskin] who do not shrink from the proposition that every object ought to be beautiful', but is adamant that such a proposition would not be acceptable in the scholastic system.
In his Paris Notebooks (1903) and Pola Notebooks (1904), Joyce has set out the basis for the conversations on beauty which occur in *A Portrait* and *Stephen Hero*. These notes can give us an insight as to how at the outset he was off course in his attempt to interpret Aquinas's aesthetic.

If the activity of simple perception is, like every other activity, itself pleasant, every sensible object that has been apprehended can be said in the first place to have been and to be in a measure beautiful; and even the most hideous object can be said to have been and to be beautiful in so far as it has been apprehended. In regard then to that part of the act of apprehension which is called the activity of simple perception there is no sensible object which cannot be said to be in a measure beautiful. [Pola Notebooks of James Joyce

(1904), quoted in James Joyce, *The Critical Writings*, edited by Ellsworth Mason and Richard Ellmann, Viking, 1972]

For Aquinas the last sentence would be acceptable in the ontological sense but not the epistemological one. In the mind of the Creator there is no object which cannot attain to the beautiful as it is perceived in the context of a universal awareness, a process not achievable by the finite mind.

3. *The Notebooks and Papers of Gerard Manley Hopkins*, edited by Humphry House (1937), p.98 et seq.

4. Ibid., p.143

5. Ibid., p.161

6. W.H. Gardner, *Gerard Manley Hopkins* (London: Secker & Warburg, 1944), p.25

7. 'It is impossible to abstract universals from the singular without previous knowledge of the singular; for in this case the intellect would abstract without knowing from what it was abstracting.' Duns Scotus: *Questiones de Anima XXII*

8. Aquinas, *Gent.* 1.51. 'Since they are intrinsically dependent on each other, the two essential principles of being exist only in virtue of their union. The primary exigence of matter is to receive a profound, specific impress, an essential form, in order that it may become some specific kind of body. The form, on its part, is essentially nothing but the determination of its potential subject matter, which from being merely potential it makes definite and actual. *Together they make up one complete essence*, one basic principle of action, a single material being.' D. Nys, STB, PhD. In Cardinal Mercier, *A Manual of Modern Scholastic Philosophy* (London: Kegan Paul, Trench, Trubner and Co. Ltd, 1921)

Select Bibliography

Adamnan, St, *see* Huyshe

Baldick, Robert, ed. and trans., *Pages from the Goncourt Journal*, New York: Oxford University Press, 1978

Barker, Richard H., *Marcel Proust: A Biography*, New York: Grosset and Dunlap, 1958

Barnes, Julian, *Flaubert's Parrot*, London: Pan Books, 1985

Beckett, Samuel, *Proust*, New York: Grove Press, 1931

Behan, Brendan, *Confessions of an Irish Rebel*, London: Hutchinson, 1965

Bell, Quentin, *Virginia Woolf: A Biography*, London: The Hogarth Press, 1972

Boswell, James, *The Life of Johnson*, London: Penguin, 1979. (First published 1791)

Bugliosi, Vincent, with Curt Gentry, *Helter Skelter – The True Story of the Manson Murders*, New York: W. W. Norton, 1974

Camus, Albert, *The Outsider*, trans. Joseph Laredo, London: Penguin, 1983. (First published 1942)

Capote, Truman, *In Cold Blood*, London: Abacus, 1984. (First published 1966)

—— *Music for Chameleons*, New York: New American Library, 1987

Clarke, Gerald, *Capote: A Biography*, London: Hamish Hamilton, 1988

Clifford, James L., *From Puzzles to Portraits, Problems of a Literary Biographer*, Chapel Hill: University of North Carolina Press, 1970

—— In *Studies in Biography*, 'Hanging up Looking Glasses at Odd Corners: Ethnobiographical Prospects'

Clifford, James L., ed., *Biography as an Art*, New York: Oxford University Press, 1962

Cockshut, A. O. J., *Truth to Life: The Art of Biography in the Nineteenth Century*, London: Collins: 1974

Select Bibliography

Cooper-Prichard, A. H., *Conversations with Oscar Wilde*, London: Philip Allan, 1931

Coplestone, Frederick, S. J., *A History of Philosophy*, Vol. I, 1946; Vol. II, 1950; Vol. III, 1953, London: Burns, Oates and Washbourne

Corvo, Baron (Fr. Rolfe), *Hadrian the Seventh*, London: Chatto and Windus, 1929

Crick, Bernard, *George Orwell*, London: Penguin, 1982

Croft-Cooke, Rupert, *Feasting with Panthers*, London: W. H. Allen, 1967

de Vere White, Terence, *A Fretful Midge*, London: Routledge and Kegan Paul, 1959

Dick, Oliver Lawson, ed., *Aubrey's Brief Lives*, London: Penguin, 1982

Dickson, Albert, ed., *Sigmund Freud*, Volume 14 – 'Art and Literature', London: Penguin, 1985

Doctorow, E. L., *Ragtime*, London: Pan Books, 1976

Edel, Leon, *Writing Lives (Principia Biographica)*, New York and London: W. W. Norton, 1984

Ellmann, Richard, *Along the Riverside*, London: Hamish Hamilton, 1988

—— *James Joyce*, new and revised edition, London and New York: Oxford University Press, 1982

—— *Oscar Wilde*, London: Hamish Hamilton, 1987

Ellmann, Richard, ed., *Selected Letters of James Joyce*, London: Faber and Faber, 1975

Empson, William, 'Using Biography', *New Statesman Review*, 31 October 1959

Field, Andrew, *Nabokov: His Life in Part*, London: Penguin, 1978

Finney, Brian, *The Inner I*, London: Faber and Faber, 1985

Foot, Michael, *The Politics of Paradise: A Vindication of Byron*, London: Collins, 1988

Furbank, P. N., *E. M. Forster: A Life*, Oxford University Press, 1979

Gardner, W. H., *Gerard Manley Hopkins*, London: Secker and Warburg, 1944

Gogarty, Oliver St John, *As I was Going Down Sackville Street*, London: Rich and Cowan, 1937

Gosse, Edmund, *Father and Son*, London: Penguin, 1983

—— *The Life of Philip Henry Gosse FRS*, London: Kegan Paul, Trench, Trübner, 1890

Guiles, Fred Lawrence, *Norma Jean: The Life of Marilyn Monroe*, London: W. H. Allen, 1969

Hamblett, Charles, *Who Killed Marilyn Monroe?*, London: Leslie Frewin, 1966

Harding, James, *Agate: A Biography*, London: Methuen, 1986.

Hart, Charles, ed., *Aspects of the New Scholastic Philosophy*, (Associates and former Pupils of Dr Edward A. Pace), New York: Benziger Bros, 1932

Hemmings, F. W. J., *Baudelaire the Damned: A Biography*, London: Hamish Hamilton, 1982

Holmes, Richard, *Footsteps*, London: Hodder and Stoughton, 1985

Holroyd, Michael, *Lytton Strachey: A Biography*, London: Penguin, 1980

—— *Unreceived Opinions*, London: Heinemann, 1973

—— *Augustus John*, London: Heinemann, 1974/5

Homberger, Eric, and Charmley, John, *The Troubled Face of Biography*, London: Macmillan, 1988

Huyshe, Wentworth, trans., *The Life of St Columba by St Adamnan AD 679–704*, London: George Routledge and Sons, 1905

John, Augustus, *Autobiography*, with an introduction by Michael Holroyd, London: Jonathan Cape, 1975

Joyce, James, *A Portrait of the Artist as a Young Man*, London: Penguin, 1960. (First published 1916)

—— *Ulysses*, London: Penguin, 1972. (First published 1922)

Karl, Frederick R., *Modern and Modernism: The Sovereignty of the Artist 1885–1925*, London and New York: Atheneum, 1985

Kavanagh, Patrick, *The Green Fool*, London: Michael Joseph, 1938

Kavanagh, Peter, *Sacred Keeper: A Biography of Patrick Kavanagh*, The Goldsmith Press, 1979

Keeler, Christine, and Meadley, Robert, *Sex Scandals*, London: Xanadu Publications, 1985

Kenner, Hugh, 'The Impertinence of Being Definitive', in *Times Literary Supplement*, 17 December 1982

Krause, Charles A., *Guyana Massacre: The Eyewitness Account*, London: Pan Books, 1979

MacCarthy, Desmond, *Experience*, London: Putnam, 1935

—— *Memories*, London: MacGibbon and Kee, 1953

Mailer, Norman, *Advertisements for Myself*, London: Panther, Granada Publishing, 1985

—— *An American Dream*, London: Grafton Books, 1972

—— *Marilyn*, New York: Grosset and Dunlap, 1973

—— *Miami and the Siege of Chicago*, London: Penguin, 1969. (First published 1968)

—— *The Executioner's Song*, London: Hutchinson, 1979
—— *The Presidential Papers*, London: Corgi Books, 1964
Mangiello, Dominick, *Joyce's Politics*, London: 1980
Maritain, Jacques, *Art and Scholasticism*, trans. J. F. Scanlan, London: Sheed and Ward, 1930
Maurois, André, *Ariel*, London: Penguin, 1985. (First published 1924)
—— *A Private Universe*, trans. Hamish Miles, London: Cassell, 1932
—— *The Quest for Proust*, trans. Gerard Hopkins, London: Penguin, 1962
—— *Aspects of Biography*, trans. S. C. Roberts, Cambridge University Press, 1929
—— *Call No Man Happy*, trans. Denver and Jane Lindley, London: The Reprint Society, 1944
—— *Disraeli*, New York: D. Appleton and Company, 1928
—— *Memoirs, 1884–1957*, London: The Bodley Head, 1970
—— *Victor Hugo*, trans. Gerard Hopkins, London: Jonathan Cape, 1956
Meyers, Jeffrey, ed., *The Biographer's Art: New Essays*, University of Colorado, 1989
—— *The Craft of Literary Biography*, 1985
Miller, Henry, *The Time of the Assassins: A Study of Rimbaud*, New York: New Directions, 1962
Mills, Hilary, *Mailer: A Biography*, London: New English Library, 1982
Moore, George, *A Mummer's Wife*, London: Heinemann, 1933
—— *Confessions of a Young Man*, London: Penguin, 1939. (First published 1918)
—— *Conversations in Ebury Street*, London: Chatto and Windus, 1969
—— *Hail and Farewell*, Gerrards Cross: Colin Smythe, 1976
—— *Impressions and Opinions*, London: David Nutt, 1891
—— *The Untilled Field*, London: Heinemann, 1931
Moore, Thomas, *Memoirs of ... Richard Brinsley Sheridan*, Chicago, 1882
Morgan, Charles, *Epitaph on George Moore*, New York: Macmillan, 1935
Morley, John, *Life of Gladstone*, Vols I, II and III, London: Macmillan, 1903, 1904
Murphy, Gerard, 'The Nature of Poets', in *Irish Ecclesiastical Record* (August 1945), pp. 93 et seq. (November 1946)
Nadel, Ira Bruce, *Biography, Fiction, Fact and Form*, 1984
Nicolson, Harold, *The Development of English Biography*, New York: 1929

Noon, William T., S.J., *Joyce and Aquinas*, New Haven and London: Yale University Press, 1957

O'Connor, Ulick, *Brendan Behan*, London: Hamish Hamilton, 1970

—— *Oliver St John Gogarty: A Biography*, London: Jonathan Cape, 1964

Painter, George D., *Marcel Proust: A Biography*, London: Penguin, 1983

Plutarch, *Makers of Rome*, trans. Ian Scott-Kilvert, London: Penguin, 1987

Potts, William, ed., *James Joyce: Portraits of the Artist in Exile*, Dublin: Wolfhound Press, 1979

Powell, Anthony, *John Aubrey and his Friends*, London: The Hogarth Press, 1988

Proust, Marcel, *By Way of Sainte-Beuve*, trans. Sylvia Townsend Warner, London: Chatto and Windus, 1958

—— *Cities of the Plain*, Part I, London: Chatto and Windus, 1968

—— *Swann's Way*, Part II, trans. C. K. Scott Moncrieff, London: Chatto and Windus, 1970

Purcell, Edmond Sheridan, *Life of Cardinal Manning, Archbishop of Westminster*, 2 vols, 1896.

Ransome, Arthur, *Oscar Wilde*, London: Methuen, 1913. (First published by Martin Secker, 1912)

Raphael, Frederick, *Byron*, London: Thames and Hudson, 1982

Richardson, Joanna, *Théophile Gautier*, London: Max Reinhardt, 1958

Rolfe, Fr., *see* Corvo

Ross, Lillian, *Picture*, London: Penguin, 1962. (First published 1952)

Rousseau, Jean-Jacques, *The Confessions*, trans. J. M. Cohen. London: Penguin, 1953

Ruitenbeek, Hendrik M., ed., *Freud, As We Knew Him*, Detroit: Wayne State University Press, 1973

Russell, Bertrand, *A History of Western Philosophy*, London: Unwin Paperbacks, 1979

Ryan, John, *Remembering How We Stood*, Dublin: Gill and Macmillan, 1975

Salmagundi: A Quarterly of the Humanities and Social Sciences, Skidmore College, New York, 1983

Scheikevitch, Maric, *Times Past: Memories of Proust and Others*, trans. Françoise Delisle, Boston: Houghton Mifflin Co., 1935

Sitwell, Osbert, *Great Morning*, London: Macmillan, 1948

—— *Laughter in the Next Room*, London: Macmillan, 1949

—— *Left Hand, Right Hand!*, London: Macmillan, 1945

—— *Noble Essences*, London: Macmillan, 1950

—— *The Scarlet Tree*, London: Macmillan, 1946

Starkie, Enid, *Baudelaire*, New York: New Directions, 1958

Stone, Irving, *The Agony and the Ecstasy*, London: Methuen, 1987. (First published 1961)

Strachey, Lytton, *Elizabeth and Essex*, London: Chatto and Windus, 1928

—— *Eminent Victorians*, New York: The Modern Library, 1918

—— *Queen Victoria*, London: Chatto and Windus, 1921

Strong, L.A.G., *The Minstrel Boy: A Portrait of Tom Moore*, London: Hodder and Stoughton, 1937

Symons, A.J.A., *The Quest for Corvo*, London: Penguin, 1940

Symons, Julian, *A.J.A. Symons: His Life and Speculations*, Oxford University Press, 1986

Thwaite, Ann, *Edmund Gosse: A Literary Landscape, 1849–1928*, London: Secker and Warburg, 1984

Wallace, Irving, *The Prize*. London: New English Library, 1961

Whibley, Charles, 'The Limits of Biography' in *Biography as an Art*, 1987.

Wilson, Edmund, *Axel's Castle*, London: Collins, Fontana, 1959

Winslow, Donald J, *Life-Writing*, Hawaii: The University Press, 1980

Woolf, Leonard, *The Journey Not the Arrival Matters*, London: The Hogarth Press, 1970

Woolf, Leonard, ed, *A Writer's Diary: Being Extracts from the Diary of Virginia Woolf*, London: Hogarth Press, 1953

Woolf, Virginia, *Granite and Rainbow*, 1958

—— *Mrs. Dalloway*, London: Panther, 1976. (First published 1925)

—— *Orlando, A Biography*, London: Penguin Books, 1967

Yeats, W.B., *Autobiographies*, London: Macmillan, 1955

The following two excellent studies by Umberto Eco were published in the UK after I had completed this book, and they are not therefore included in the bibliography: *The Middle Ages of James Joyce*, London: Hutchinson Radius, 1989 and *The Aesthetics of Thomas Aquinas*, Radius, 1988. Michael Holroyd's three-volume biography of George Bernard Shaw is not included for the same reason.

Index

A La Recherche du Temps Perdu (Proust), 70–1, 80
Agony and the Ecstasy, The (Stone), 95
American Dream, An (Mailer), 29–30
Anrep, Helen, 63
Aquinas, St Thomas, 12, 108–9, 113
Armies of the Night (Mailer), 24, 33, 36, 39
Arnold, Thomas, 92
As I Was Going Down Sackville Street (Gogarty), 102
Atheneum, 89
Atkin, Susan, 28
Aubrey, John, 2-3
Augustus John (Holroyd), 23

Baker, Nicole, 29, 30, 32
Balzac, Honoré, 9–10
Baudelaire, C. P., xi, 105
Beckett, Samuel, 18, 71, 104
Behan, Brendan, 93
  arrest of, 114-26
  O'Connor biography, 97–100

Behan, Dominic, 98–9
Behan, Kathleen, 99
Bell, Quentin, 63
Bell, Vanessa, 63
Benson, E. F., 47
Best, Richard, 72, 78
Blunt, Wilfrid, 95
Bonaparte, Napoleon, 6, 81
Boswell, James, 2, 3
Bowles, Paul, xii–xiii
Brenan, Gerald, 20, 21
Brief Lives (Aubrey), 2
Brummell, Beau, 81, 82
Buckley, Joseph, 115, 118
Burger, Chief Justice, 34
Burroughs, William, 24
Byron, George, Lord, 4, 7, 46–7, 63, 105

Camus, Albert, xi, 105–6
Capote, Truman, 36–9
Carpenter, Edward, 64
Carrington, Dora, 20
Cawthorne, Dr Terence, 56–7
Chamber Music (Joyce), 15
Clarke, Austin, 93
Clifford, James L., 11–12
Clutter, Nancy, 38

Index

Colum, Padraic, 92
Confessions of a Young Man
 (Moore), 80
Confessions of an Irish Rebel
 (Behan), 115–26
Conmee, Fr., SJ, 72
Contemporary Review, The, 80
Coppola, Francis Ford, 31
Corr, Jack, 124
Corso, Gregory, 24
Cosgrave, Vincent, 79
Countess Cathleen, The
 (Yeats), 85
Cummins, Jim, 123
Cutting of an Agate, The
 (Yeats), 89

Darwin, Charles, 54, 106
Daudet, Alphonse, 48
Degas, E., 80
Dewey, Alvin, 38
Dickens, Charles, 4
Dodd, Reuben, 72, 75, 76
Donegan, Det. Garda Jim, 117,
 119, 125
Donleavy, J. P., 29
Doran, Det., 117, 119, 125
Dostoevsky, F. M., 105
Dramatis Personae (Yeats), 87
Dubliners(Joyce), 80
Duns Scotus, 108, 111, 112–3
Dunton, Theodore Watts, 51

Eglington, John, 72
Eliot, T. S., 23, 89
Elizabeth and Essex (Strachey),
 8, 22
Elliott, George P., 28
Ellmann, Prof. Richard, 53–8
 Joyce biography, 13–19
 Wilde biography, 55–8
Eminent Victorians (Strachey),
 8, 10, 22, 58
Evening Telegraph, 73

Executioner's Song, The
 (Mailer), 28–36

Father and Son (Gosse), 65–9
Ferlinghetti, Lawrence, 24
Finnegans Wake (Joyce), 17
Fitzgerald, Scott, 37
Flaherty, Dick, 115, 116, 117,
 120, 123
Flaubert, Gustave, 48
Forster, E. M., 62
Forster, J., 4
Frank, Nino, 17–18
Freeman's Journal, 72–4, 76
Freud, Sigmund, 52–3, 106
Fry, Roger, 63–5

Gabler, Prof. Hans W., 78
Gautier, Théophile, 105
Gertler, Mark, 20
Gilmore, Gary, 28–36
Ginger Man, The (Donleavy),
 29
Ginsberg, Allen, 24
Gladstone, W. E., 4–7
Goethe, J. W. von, 52
Gogarty, Martha Duane, 100
Gogarty, Oliver St John, 54–5,
 79, 92, 97
 O'Connor biography, 100–2
Goncourt brothers, 47–9
Gonne, Maud, 94, 95
Goodwin, Det. Garda, 119
Gordon, General, 10, 58, 92
Gosse, Edmund, 47–51, 59,
 65–9, 104
Great Morning (Sitwell), 40
Green Fool, The (Kavanagh),
 101-2
Gregan, Paul, 15
Gregory, Lady, 83, 86, 87,
 88, 93, 95
Griffith, Jackie, 122
Guiles, Fred, 26

Hail and Farewell (Moore),
  80–7, 88, 104
Hanrahan, Det. Martin,
  117, 118–19
Hersey, J. R., 40
Higgins, F. R., 93
Hobbs, 46
Holmes, John Clelland, 24
Holroyd, Michael, 19–24
Hopkins, Gerard Manley, 107,
  108, 111–13
Huston, John, 39
Hyde, Douglas, 94

Ibsen, Henrik, 105
In Cold Blood (Capote), 36–9
Irish Independent, 75
Irish Literary Renaissance,
  83–9, 92–6
Irish Worker, 76

James, Henry, 37
James Joyce (Ellmann), 53–5
John, Augustus, 23
Johnson, Peter, 58
Johnson, Dr Samuel, 11
Jones, James, xii–xiii, 105
Joyce, James, 23, 62, 69, 80, 92
  and Beckett, 18
  compared with Proust, 70–2
  creation of aesthetic,
    107–11, 113
  Ellmann biography, 13–19,
    53–55
  use of reality in *Ulysses*,
    71–80
Joyce, John Stanislaus, 16–17

Kael, Pauline, 26
Karl, Frederick, 106
Kavanagh, Patrick, 93, 101–2
Kelly, Mick, 121
Kennedy, Robert, 27–8
Kenner, Hugh, 19, 53, 55

Kerouac, Jack, 24
Kidwell, Susan, 38
Kiely, Benedict, 93, 98
Killeen, Jim, 122
Kingsmill, Hugh, 19
Kirwan, Det., 119
Kolb, Philip, 70

Lake, The (Moore), 79, 86
Larkin, Jim, 76
Laughter in the Next Room
  (Sitwell), 40
Lavin, Mary, 93
Lawrence, D. H., 17, 23
Lee, Sir Sidney, 19
Left Hand, Right Hand!
  (Sitwell), 40
Leigh, Augusta, 46
Lewis, Wyndham, 23
*Life of Philip Henry Gosse
  FRS, The* (Gosse), 65–6
Lockhart, J. G., 3–4

Macaulay, T. B., 4
MacCarthy, Desmond,
  38, 69, 94
McCool, Sean, 122
MacNamara, Desmond,
  99–100
Mailer, Norman, 23–36,
  38, 39–40
  Monroe biography, 24, 25–8
Mallarmé, Stéphane, 105
Manet, E., 80, 88
Mangan, Lazarian, 115, 116
Mangan, Seamus, 116, 119–20,
  125
Manning, Cardinal, 10,
  21, 67, 92
Manson, Charles, 28
Manzoni, A., 6
Marilyn (Mailer), 24, 25–8
Martyn, Edward, 82, 83, 93
Maupassant, Guy de, 47–9, 50

Index

Maurois, André, 9–10, 11, 14, 19, 23
Meersam, Fr., 32
Mercier, D., 110
Miami and the Siege of Chicago (Mailer), 33
Miller, Arthur, 26
Mills, Hilary, 30
Moate, Henry, 45
Monroe, Marilyn, 24, 25–7
Moore, George, 66, 78, 79, 93, 104
 Hail and Farewell, 80–7
 Yeats on, 87–8
Moore, Thomas, 4, 7, 46
More, Sir Thomas, 2–3
Morgan, Charles, 88
Morley, John, 4–7
Mummer's Wife, A (Moore), 80
Murphy, Mary Ellen, 29
Murray, Eunice, 26
Murray (publisher), 46
Muses are Heard, The (Capote), 36–7
Music for Chameleons (Capote), 36

Naked and the Dead, The (Mailer), 24
Nathan, Andrew, 115, 118
Newman, Cardinal, 21, 67
Nhu, Madame, 28
Nichol, Brenda, 31
Nicolson, Harold, 59, 61
Nietzsche, F. W., 106
Nightingale, Florence, 92
Nijinsky, Vaslav, 105
Nys, D., 113

O'Brien, Flann, 93
O'Casey, Sean, 92
O'Connell, John, 72
O'Connor, Donal, 121
O'Connor, Frank, 93

Of a Fire on the Moon (Mailer), 39
O'Faolain, Sean, 93
O'Flaherty, Liam, 93
O'Grady, Standish, 94
O'Leary, John, 94
O'Neill, Ultan, 116
Orlando (Woolf), 59–62, 65, 104
Oscar Wilde (Ellmann), 55–8
O'Sullivan, Seumas, 92
Outsider, The (Camus), 106

Painter, George, 51–2, 70–2
Pater, Walter, 92
Peste, La (Camus), 106
Picture (Ross), 39
Plunkett, Horace, 94
Plunkett, James, 93
Plutarch, 2, 17
Portrait of the Artist as a Young Man, A (Joyce), 80, 108–9
Pound, Ezra, 51
Power, Arthur, 17
Proust, Marcel, 9, 40, 45, 52, 80, 104
 Joyce compared with, 70–2
Pulchrum et bonum, 12–15, 23, 107–8

Quearney, Martin, 116
Queen Victoria (Strachey), 8, 22

Ransome, Arthur, 55, 56–7
Ravenna, Bishop of, 1
Recreant (Gregan), 15
Rembrandt, 14
Remembrance of Times Past (Proust), 70–2, 80
Rimbaud, A., 24, 105
Ritter, Judge, 34
Robinson, Lennox, 92–3

Roper, Sir William, 3
Ross, Lillian, 39
Rousseau, Jean Jacques,
　xi, 4, 105
Ruby, Jack, 28
Russell, George (AE), 82,
　83, 86, 92
Ryan, Cornelius, 40

Sackville-West, Vita, 59–61
Scarlet Tree, The (Sitwell), 40
Schenk, Joseph, 27
Schiller, Laurence, 25,
　28–9, 31, 33
Scott, Sir Walter, 3, 4
Shaw, George Bernard, 94
Shawn, William, 37
Shelley, Percy Bysshe, 9
Sheridan, Richard Brinsley, 4
Sitwell, Sir George, 40–5
Sitwell, Osbert, 23, 43–5, 104
Souvenirs sur James Joyce
　(Frank), 17–19
Stephens, James, 92
Stone, Irving, 95
Strachey, James, 19–20
Strachey, Lytton, 9, 10, 11,
　14, 19, 94
　Holroyd biography
　　of, 19–22
　theory of biography, 8, 23,
　　58, 67, 90, 92
Stuart, Francis, 93
Suarez, F. de, 111
Summa Theologica (Aquinas),
　108, 110
Sunset Town (Gregan), 15
Swift, Jonathan, 18
Swinburne, A. G., 47–51, 69
Swinburne, Isobel, 51
Symonds, John Addington, 51,
　64
Symons, Arthur, 94
Synge, J. M., 78, 86, 89, 92

Tatarkiewiez, Prof., 112
Tennyson, Alfred Lord,
　4, 46, 63
Thrift, H. V. (Harry), 74, 78–9
Tolstoy, L., 81
Tomlin, Stephen, 22
Trefusis, Violet, 61
Trevelyan, G. M., 4
Turner, Reginald, 56
Tynan, Kenneth, 37

Ulysses (Joyce), 45, 54–5, 62
　reality in, 71–80
Untilled Field, The (Moore),
　80, 86

Vain Fortune (Moore), 80
Verlaine, Paul, 80
Victoria, Queen, 50
Voltaire, F. M. A. de, xi, 4

Wallace, Mike, 26
Weaver, Harriet, 16
White Negro, The (Mailer), 24
Wilde, Oscar, 55–8, 78, 94
Wilmot, Det. Garda Richard,
　119
Wolfe, Tom, 40
Woolf, Leonard, 63
Woolf, Virginia, 19, 37,
　46, 51, 96
　Fry biography, 63–5
　Orlando, 59–62, 104
Wordsworth, William, 4
Wreck of the Deutschland
　(Hopkins), 112

Yeats, W. B., 92, 95
　by Moore, 82–7
　on Moore, 87–9

Zola, Emile, 88
Zolotow, Maurice, 26